CURRICULUM EVALUATION
FOR SCHOOL IMPROVEMENT

CURRICULUM EVALUATION
FOR SCHOOL
IMPROVEMENT

By

JOHN C. HILL, Ph.D.

Department of Educational Administration
University of Cincinnati
Cincinnati, Ohio

CHARLES C THOMAS • PUBLISHER
Springfield • Illinois • U.S.A.

Published and Distributed Throughout the World by

CHARLES C THOMAS • PUBLISHER
2600 South First Street
Springfield, Illinois 62717

© *1986 by* CHARLES C THOMAS • PUBLISHER

ISBN 0-398-05246-8

Library of Congress Catalog Card Number: 86-5707

Printed in the United States of America
SC-R-3

Library of Congress Cataloging-in-Publication Data

Hill, John C.
  Curriculum evaluation for school improvement.

  Bibliography: p.
  Includes index.
    1. Curriculum evaluation.   2. Curriculum planning.
  3. School improvement programs.   I. Title.
  LB1570.H55 1986   375'.006   86-5707
  ISBN 0-398-05246-8

For John, David, and Mai

CONTRIBUTOR

Raymond R. Spaulding, Ed.D.
Principal
Grandview Elementary School
Bellevue, Kentucky

PREFACE

This book is designed for the study and practice of curriculum evaluation. Its conceptual basis is authoritative and suitable for use in college and university courses in curriculum and evaluation. Its description of procedures and actual cases also makes it of practical value for principals, supervisors, department heads, and directors of curriculum. The book brings theory and practice into a bonded whole as head and tail of the same coin. The assumption is that the student of curriculum evaluation and the worker conducting curriculum evaluation are both concerned with an integration of theoretical perspectives and practical applications. Whichever way the coin falls, creative action and sound theory are reflexive in the educator concerned with curriculum evaluation. The purpose of the text is to bring together the professional areas of *curriculum and evaluation;* to address the dimensions of *theory and practice;* to set forth a first priority for *evaluation as meaning making* rather than the other important purposes of accountability, decision making, and program intervention.

Curriculum as a field of study has been classified in three different theory perspectives. First, control theory, which is that view of curriculum as an engineered system which is deductively developed from classic sources of learner, society, and subject discipline, and to which students will be expected to respond. Second, praxis theory, which is that view of curriculum as developed by working in the schools and in the classrooms with regular reflection on practice and research to provide meaning for development and improvement of the learning environment of students. Third, interpretive theory, which is an analytical approach to curriculum where deep structure, social/political bias, and oppressive or controlling practices are teased out and aired as criticism of schooling and education.

The first theory base, control theory, has been most used, and sensibly so, to attempt to create standard and effective schooling for everyone. Curriculum evaluation as a field to date has largely been concerned with the measurement, accountability, and rational approach to decision making which would complement this very useful if somewhat deductive and rational approach to curriculum development.

Curriculum in the praxis tradition, practice into theory into practice, is the intuitive and low technical approach, which makes great sense to teachers, principals, and educators who must make sense or meaning of the learning environment for the actual and individual learners they meet. This meaning making, fitting, and improvement of the learning program is the approach taken in this work on curriculum evaluation. It can, to be sure, be used to understand and deal with the accountability of standard approaches to curriculum development and implementation, but its central assumption is that educators responsible for a school or program can use practical steps and procedures to make meaning and so plan for the change and improvement of the curriculum.

The definition of curriculum used as a basis for this book on evaluation includes the systemic and related nature of learning, instruction, curriculum, and staff development. This is more a figure-ground perspective of curriculum than a logical-linear one. The effect of this choice of definition is to require a consideration of several influences in the curriculum at the same time.

The book has several distinctive features. It sets forth a comprehensive curriculum design of four phases: inquiry, basic skills, remediation, and self and social development. It relates the learner experience, instruction, curriculum design, materials, and staff development as the interacting components of a complete curriculum system. It relates evaluation procedures to this perspective of curriculum phases and components. The perspective of evaluation taken here is one of making meaning and not just providing data. Making meaning is a people process which can influence understanding, behavior, and growth. Thus, curriculum evaluation is proposed as a way to influence curriculum change through changes in people.

This is a textbook, not a cookbook. There are no packaged curriculum evaluation recipes found here which can be applied one-for-one to a unique classroom, course, or school. Sound perspectives, procedures, and dynamic case studies are presented which point the way for the curriculum student and worker to design and carry out tailor-made evaluations for their own curriculum setting.

Part I is titled Perspectives for Curriculum Evaluation. The five chapters in this section deal with frameworks for describing, explaining, and understanding curriculum evaluation. The contents of this section include the following: a perspective of curriculum design, the concept of evaluation as feedback, fourteen perennial issues in curriculum evaluation, and the optional models available as guides for curriculum evaluation.

Part II is titled Procedures for Curriculum Evaluation. This section reviews components and suggests steps of the curriculum evaluation procedure. It includes the following: a means to assess whether the curriculum is actually implemented or merely superficial, how to begin with a question, the use of an evaluation design matrix, sampling procedures, optional methods for data collection, selecting or creating instruments, analyzing information, making meaning, and assessing the worth of an evaluation process.

Part III is titled Practices in Curriculum Evaluation. In this section three cases of curriculum evaluations are presented which follow the responsive model and the decision-making model. These descriptions suggest the dynamic and personal quality of the actual conduct of a curriculum evaluation.

The concepts, procedures, and cases are applicable to curriculum evaluation at every level of schooling, every subject area, and are relevant to individual classrooms, complete courses, or whole school programs. The purpose of curriculum evaluation as meaning making is ultimately to contribute to understanding and potential for improvement of the teaching environment and the learner's experience in school.

ACKNOWLEDGMENTS

This is to recognize the publishers and organizations which gave permission to include pertinent materials from their works, including:

Phi Delta Kappa, Bloomington, Indiana

Educational Testing Service, Princeton, New Jersey

F.E. Peacock Publishers, Itasca, Illinois

John Wiley and Sons, New York, New York

American Educational Research Association, Washington, D.C.

Association for Supervision and Curriculum Development, Alexandria, Virginia

The Joint Committee on Standards for Educational Evaluation, c/o The Evaluation Center, Western Michigan University

Association of Secondary School Principals, Reston, Virginia

This is to acknowledge the efforts and insights of the educators and students who participated in dynamic evaluation experiences described here and in particular the skills of planning, organizing, and personal relationship qualities contributed by Rick Kohler, Steven Hawley, and Raymond Spaulding.

The critical assistance with the writing by John Daresh, Ph.D., professional colleague and faculty member of the Ohio State University, was instrumental, timely, and most appreciated.

CONTENTS

CURRICULUM EVALUATION
FOR SCHOOL IMPROVEMENT

Part I

PERSPECTIVES FOR CURRICULUM EVALUATION

Chapter 1

EVALUATION AND THE CURRICULUM

As a result of this chapter, the reader should be able to:

1. Define and give a rationale for curriculum evaluation in the tradition of meaning making.
2. Describe general steps of the deductive and the inductive procedures of curriculum development and tell how they might relate to each other.
3. Explain the problems and potentials for conducting curriculum evaluation in today's schools.
4. State the four functions of evaluation in schools.
5. Paraphrase six general guidelines to follow when conducting curriculum evaluation as meaning making.

The purpose of the curriculum of the school is to arrange for the situations, materials, and processes by which learners can engage in activities which will promote new meaning, enhanced skills, and growth. The function of instruction in school is to facilitate directly and indirectly the learner's engagement with curriculum.

Curriculum evaluation gathers evidence and promotes understanding of how to bring about the optimum arrangement of the curriculum, the most skillful facilitation of instruction, and the potentials of learners in order to increase, extend, and deepen the learner's ways of knowing, valuing, acting, and growing. It is not a procedure focused only on the identification of curriculum materials and textbooks or the assessment of learner achievements according to program objectives. Rather, it is the meaning making technology which is applied to the curriculum, instruction, and learning potentials of a school. These three, curriculum, instruction, and learning, are inseparably linked in synergy as a whole system. They are the core technology, the productive functions, which are the work of the school. This comprehensive definition of curriculum evaluation is basic to conceptions of curriculum development.

CONCEPTIONS OF CURRICULUM DEVELOPMENT

Oliva (1983) has offered three models for thinking about the relationship of curriculum to instruction. One is a model showing curriculum and instruction to be basically separate and not interacting. This is in fact a *nonmodel.* Second is a model showing curriculum and instruction components to function sequentially. That is, the procedures for developing curriculum feed into the procedures for instruction and those outcomes of instruction are cycled back to the beginning steps of curriculum development. His third model represents curriculum and instruction as imbedded concentric circles representing a continuous or meshed engagement. Oliva's oversight in all this perspective making is the complete omission of the learning component. He develops a curriculum development procedure from the interacting model of curriculum and instruction which places his work (along with many curriculum theorists) in the Tylerian tradition.

Tyler's work on curriculum development (1949) is based upon four fundamental questions:

1. What should the purposes of schools be in our society?
2. By what means can learning occur to attain those purposes?
3. What are the optimum conditions under which these means of learning can be undertaken?
4. How can we know if learning has occurred?

Tyler's curriculum development process begins with a study of needs in three areas: a study of society, a study of learners, and a study of the content area of discipline. From these three sources, needs are identified and analyzed (filtered) through a screen of educational philosophy to determine which needs are to be the prerogative of the school and through a second screen of knowledge and assumptions about learning psychology to determine which needs can be taught through the formal learning processes peculiar to the business of schools. The needs thus determined by the screening processes are then developed as educational objectives.

These objectives form the answer to the first of the four questions above. The steps through the next three questions are primarily an instructional systems process to determine what students know before instruction (preassessment), optional ways to learning the objective (appropriate means), environments and reinforcement for learning (optimum conditions), and assessment of outcomes (determining if learning has occurred). These procedures are addressed by many curriculum workers such as Popham, Baker, Saylor and Alexander, Banathy, Beauchamp, and many others. This tradition of curriculum development has come to be known as *control theory* for its emphasis on engineering of a system of curriculum and instruction to which learners respond and adapt to their ultimate benefit as members of the society. The emphasis of this tradition of curriculum development is said to be control in form because it is deductive, it determines a comprehensive design to which the learners respond.

Curriculum evaluation must address curriculum, instruction, and learning in this tradition of Tyler and others because it is a widely accepted and useful method of working with school programs. Curriculum, instruction, and learning to be developed and improved must have the feedback of a working curriculum evaluation system.

A second tradition in curriculum development derives from the inductive approach so well articulated by Hilda Taba (1962). Taba proposed a development of units of study for try-out based on eight steps which begin with a diagnosis of learner needs. This direct interaction with the learners is followed by formulation of objectives, selection of content, organization of content, selection of learning activities, organization of learning activities, selection of evaluation approaches, and a check of unit balance and sequence.

This first step of developing a pilot unit is followed by testing of the experimental unit. The testing leads to unit revisions. Once a number of units have reached the revision stage, a framework for the units is developed which would include a scope and sequence for the units and an overall rationale. A final step for this curriculum development process is the appropriate inservice training and staff development support necessary to install and disseminate the curriculum in classrooms.

Unit curriculum development and the tradition referred to as the emergent curriculum are the main approaches of which Taba has written so well. This tradition in the curriculum theory literature belongs in the domain of interactive theory or *praxis theory*. That is, the curriculum worker brings theory and practice together in the working setting and crafts the curriculum out of the interaction of real settings with a good grasp of concepts and constructs of his or her professional training. This interactive approach is described as meaning making from theory and practice.

The discussion of deep structure of curriculum development traditions is concluded by noting that there is a third category called interpretive or hermeneutic theory which presently does not offer much working approach or practice relationship to curriculum development or curriculum evaluation in schools.

The deductive curriculum development tradition (Tyler and others) and the inductive tradition by (Taba, 1962) (Unruh, 1975) (Brubaker, 1982) and others seem in the first case to represent what curriculum committee task groups do and in the second case represents what teachers working within classrooms and teaching teams do. The two approaches also suggest, each in different ways, that curriculum, instruction, and learning are intertwined. They are in fact different points in the same unified process as we shall see in Chapter 2. These approaches seem to have different fundamental purpose, one to create a design for learners to shape themselves to their future benefit and society's, and the second to construct a design out of the learners, the situation, and their needs to the benefit of the learners and their future society.

Curriculum evaluation must be considered as a perspective and procedures which will be effective in providing understanding for the development of and optimum improvement of curriculum, instruction, and learning, and must attend to these components in both traditions of curriculum development. It is the purpose of curriculum evaluation then to achieve an understanding of how the conditions of curriculum, instruction, and learner potential work to influence knowing, acting, and growth of learners. These conditions may occur as a result of either or both these curriculum development traditions.

It should also be clear that curriculum evaluation is about the process of feedback and meaning making. As curriculum evaluation gives professional educators new understanding about how curriculum, instruction, and learner potentials interact for learning to occur, we are able to remove more and more of the phenomena of curriculum and instruction from the "black box" notion.

The "black box" analogy suggests the image that we put curriculum, instruction, and learner potentials in the top slot of the box and out the bottom will come learning. If it does not result in learning, we change something about the three inputs until it comes out right. Curriculum evaluation is the tool we need to look inside the black box and begin to understand how the system works, not whether it works. Such an understanding will make curriculum change less subject to the political winds of favor and disfavor, less subject to the fads of curriculum entrepreneurs, and more subject to the professional knowledge and expertise of educators.

EVALUATION OF CURRICULUM IS NOT DONE

Curriculum evaluation is a rare activity in school, as is evaluation in general. Financial considerations for schools, the legal and regulated context of schooling, organization, and the perspective of evaluation, are some of the reasons for this lack of evaluation in schools.

School is largely a monopoly as a social institution in our society. It is, for the most part, publicly financed and governmentally regulated, much like a utility. All children must be involved or show an appropriate alternative. There is only a pittance of competition through private schools or alternatives to schooling (Raywid, 1983). Without competition, with the whole client system legally obliged to use the system, and with substantial regulation to assure the school of its identity (I am regulated, therefore I exist), there is little urgency to look to evaluation. The market has been cornered.

Financial cutbacks in education are a second factor which make the presenting of a functioning school program a legal and practical minimum. If evaluation of a school program has any financial allocation, it soon becomes subject to the cutback hit list. Evaluation is simply not viewed as an essential feature of effective functioning of schools.

Schools are not organized for curriculum evaluation. Teachers feel very little efficacy in influencing schoolwide decisions (Retsinas, 1982). They tend, without a team or consultative organization, to close the classroom door and take charge of their separate learning environments. This organizational form of school, and often the leadership which fulfills it, tends to leave teachers without perspective about the whole school and K–12 curriculum program. School sessions are scheduled for the act of instructing according to legal minimums, with little attention to planning and evaluating. That is why teachers plan lessons and grade papers at home after the school day.

Attitudes of school people, boards, and communities influence the paucity of evaluation. Community perceptions of schooling tend to fall into the following notions: schooling should not be an experiment, it should be as the parent remembers it, and it should have a certainty about it that does not require much attention to evaluation. Board members may get elected on campaigns dealing with learning, teaching, and the curriculum, but content analysis of board actions shows they spend most of their time dealing with finance and perhaps one-tenth of their time on matters of curriculum. Teachers, by viewing school as a classroom sized world in which they become the isolated adult and major actor, find the need to be a fully committed participant in the setting leaves little time to gather the evidence before them. Teacher judgments are subtle, subjective, and constant (Salmon-Cox, 1981). There is little time or support for more organized forms of curriculum evaluation.

The nature of evaluation as presently perceived is also limiting. It is often viewed as a highly technical task, separated from the teaching and learning activity, done by someone other than the school staff, largely to find out what is wrong. The reported findings seem to be communicated to a limited group and end up having no real effect on the situation (Sproull and Zubrow, 1981).

This is a rather gloomy picture of evaluation as a school function. If it were not for a few encouraging developments at hand, we might conclude that evaluation is moribund and that a thorough study of the theory and practice of curriculum evaluation is a futile effort.

POTENTIAL FOR CURRICULUM EVALUATION

One of the most encouraging signs of a growing need for curriculum evaluation is the present initiative of the Federal Department of Education to produce a "wall chart" to compare education state by state. This comparison by states uses education indicators which are most appropriate for large scale policy making. There are, in the first efforts, no indicators dealing with curriculum quality, and only general indicators about learners. This initiative (or intrusion) by the federal government into education, which is a constitutionally accepted function of individual states, is looked upon with considerable concern. It has, however, created a response by individual state departments to find a means to assess more clearly the effectiveness of schools (Shine and Goldman, 1980).

This movement to assess schools is largely based upon social-political developments, and is not motivated by professional educationists. The consequences of this movement will no doubt require professional educationists to look carefully at the function of evaluation as a tool to improve curriculum, instruction, and potentials for learning.

A second development in education which has contributed to the need for curriculum evaluation is known as the effective schools research (Curran, 1982). This work began by identifying schools which were showing a special excellence in standardized testing of their students, even though the socioeconomic factor of community and other variables would suggest that the school should be poor in educational outcomes. Studies of these schools revealed some variables which correlated with the successful outcomes. Among these were school leadership, objectives-based curricula, more available time devoted to instruction, and high expectations held by the administrator and staff for students (Edmonds, 1982) (Mackenzie, 1983). The variables which seemed to be related to the difference between effective and ineffective schools have been used in program development efforts in schools in an attempt to reproduce in a causal way the outcomes of the effective schools first identified.

The work with effective schools has been criticized as a movement based more upon political assumptions than on sound research, but it has raised educators' awareness of the potential of studying why and how schools do influence the achievements of their students (Cuban, 1983).

These approaches to school assessment seem to represent more the control theorists point of view about good curriculum and instruction. That is, we can find a general set of conditions which will largely apply to any situation and we can engineer these conditions into a school setting and cause the learners to achieve according to an external set of standards deemed to be of value, such as SAT test scores.

A third development in the field of education which represents a more interactionist theory of curriculum and instructional development is the school improvement orientation (Klausmeier, 1982). This praxis approach to improvement (more in keeping with this present work on curriculum evaluation) begins with such assumptions as the following: the single school is the unit for change and not a school district or schools in general. The beliefs, skills, and decision making of the staff of the school is central to curriculum and instructional quality. And, the school improvement effort must start with the school program where it is and be cognizant of the culture and community in which the school is situated (Goodlad, 1975).

These three major efforts to improve the quality of schooling encourage attention by educators to evaluate not only the outcomes of schooling (what happened), but why and how curriculum, instruction, and learning are effective. The "why it works," and "how it works better," questions are the central issues of curriculum evaluation, and they are the keys to optimum learning programs in schools.

THE FUNCTIONS OF EVALUATION IN SCHOOLS

There are four functions which evaluation can serve in schools. These four are not mutually exclusive functions; they overlap. These four tend to start from different assumptions. It is the treatise of the book that one of these functions should have priority and is more consistent with the perspectives, practices, and cases presented. First, one evaluation function is for accountability. Accountability is defined as to tell, explain, or justify. Evaluation for accountability is done to show that standards have been met, the school program has value, and that the actors involved (usually only the teachers) are competent. Some examples of evaluation for accountability are the annual publication of student test scores by school districts, the accreditation review which schools undergo at regular five or eight-year intervals, the certification of teachers, and the evaluation reports which are a part of funded projects such as federal title programs.

Evaluation for intervention purposes is a second function. Intervention is often undertaken through evaluation to heighten awareness about a problem and to direct a change in a school program. The recent commission (1983) which produced the report, "A Nation at Risk: The Imperative For Educational Reform," is an example of evaluation to raise awareness and to bring pressure of public attention for purposes of bringing about change.

Evaluation for decision making is a management approach undertaken by school leaders to make choices about programs based on evidence and reason. This approach is usually combined with a goal setting and annual planning approach to program development.

Evaluation for meaning making is a fourth function which is emphasized here. It has much to do with diagnosing the needs of the curriculum, instruction, and learning processes of the school. It emphasizes the inquiry by which we may find out not only that program results can be measured, but that what, why, and how questions about the program can be answered. Meaning making among the professional educators and the clients of a school has two advantages: (1) making meaning is the basis for the social interaction model of planned change. Simply put, when people change their minds, changes in behavior more easily follow.

(2) Support for school improvement is facilitated by informed professionals and clients of the school.

PRINCIPLES OF CURRICULUM EVALUATION

A principle, as used here, is a rule of thumb which can be useful to guide one's actions in many situations, much of the time. Being more prescriptive or dogmatic about a principle in the field of education which has so much work yet to do in establishing a knowledge base is not wise.

Principles are derived from four sources: generalizations supported by research, generalizations derived from theory explanations, generalizations synthesized from the wisdom of experience and practical work in the field, and generalizations which derive from common sense (Oliva, 1983).

The following are principles for the pursuit of curriculum evaluation. They are useful general guidelines for thought and action given a healthy respect for the unique nature of each situation.

1. *Changing meaning is the prerequisite to authentic changes in behavior.*

For individuals as well as groups, for teachers, administrators, parents, and students, new meaning must precede authentic changes in behavior and growth. New programs requiring new behavior, on the contrary, can be mandated, but compliant behavior is not a long-lasting or authentic form of change. Improvement of instruction as well as learning experience are based upon new meanings realized by the individuals involved. It is the function of curriculum evaluation to provide the processes for making meaning of feedback information. Information itself is not the product of curriculum evaluation; new meaning developed by each individual involved is.

Decision making based upon evaluation is usually viewed as providing information in a timely fashion in anticipation of a point in time where a choice between two alternative courses of action will be taken. Decision making in this instance is a very logical, rational, and linear construct. The dynamic condition of making a decision is usually much different.

A decision making process based on meaning making is much more like coming to a realization of what action to take. It involves carrying the information into a personal and interpersonal process of dialogue.

From this process comes a relating to past experience, a reconstruction of form, and a valuing which we can describe as meaning making.

2. *Curriculum evaluation must begin with a key question.*

The development of new meaning and realization about what actions must follow to improve a school program begins to unfold from the seed of a key question. Curriculum evaluation will quickly break away from mechanistic and *canned* procedures and evaluation models if it is based upon a key question. A question is key when it has implications for curriculum, teaching, and learning, and when it is a catalyst for dialogue among school staff. The link between key question and meaning making cannot be disregarded if curriculum evaluation is to be effective.

3. *The individual school is the primary unit for curriculum evaluation and feedback to improve curriculum, instruction, and learning.*

Those at the school must be central in designing the curriculum evaluation effort. This effort must be supported with school time and resources and must have skilled leadership and attitudinal support that the effort is important. External resources, information, and personnel are appropriate as they support the effort of the school staff.

The individual school as a unit has within it the staff linked to each other by day-to-day exigencies, by the common setting, and by the culture or ways-of-doing-things which develop almost out-of-consciousness. These are the persons who know the students in subtle detail. They not only cannot be left out of curriculum evaluation and improvement, they are the only persons who can commit their resources and energy to the teaching and learning functions of the school.

4. *Curriculum evaluation is integral to curriculum, instruction, and learning.*

An effective curriculum evaluation process for meaning making is dynamic, continuous, and integral to the technical core of schools, the curriculum, instruction, and learning. Curriculum evaluation will take a form which fits the needs of the situation and the key question which guides it. Curriculum evaluation should occur as a continual process just as instruction or learning does. Curriculum evaluation occurs in an integrated fashion. As illustrated by case studies in Section III, it is carried out as learning occurs; it occurs as instruction occurs. Evaluation which is disconnected from the core technology of the school has very little potential for meaning making.

5. *Every curriculum evaluation process is unique*

Evaluation models from the scholars in the field can be useful as orientations to the curriculum evaluation problem which one faces. If the fundamental or predominant purpose for the evaluation can be agreed upon, the several models or traditions in the evaluation field can help give guidance to the plan and conduct of the effort.

But every situation is unique; it is the crucial life situation of the persons involved. To the extent that a curriculum evaluation plan follows a model from the scholars in the field, it does not fit the real situation at hand, and to the extent that it fits the real situation at hand, it will not follow a model or a package of procedures and instruments. If the evaluation effort is fascinating to those involved and the question arises, "What is our next move?" the evaluation is responsive to the unique situation.

6. *Curriculum evaluation provides the potential for new meaning making to all persons related to the school*

Teachers and school staff are the prime movers of curriculum and instructional improvement. Their understandings resulting from the curriculum evaluation process are crucial. It should also be a part of the process to engage in developing new understandings about the school with learners, supervisors, parents, board members, and others. Every effective curriculum evaluation will include steps to involve these persons in dialogue.

SUMMARY

Curriculum development has been described in deductive approaches and inductive approaches with consequent functions of curriculum evaluation. The assumption set forth in this book is that curriculum evaluation defined as meaning making has more potential for change and improvement of the learning environment of the school.

This chapter also summarizes why curriculum evaluation is seldom, if ever, conducted in schools. Noted were restrictions related to finances, control of schools, and the educator's role. And second, why there are some unfolding changes in the curriculum field which bode well for curriculum evaluation as a central function of school improvement in the future, namely, the research on effective schools and the new national attention on schools.

Four functions of curriculum evaluation — accountability, intervention, decision making, and meaning making—are identified and described. Six general principles for curriculum evaluation are identified as: (1) Changing meaning is prerequisite to changing behavior. (2) Curriculum evaluation begins with a question. (3) The individual school is the primary unit for learning improvement. (4) Curriculum evaluation is integral with curriculum, instruction, and learning. (5) Every curriculum evaluation process is unique. (6) New meaning is important to all persons related to the school.

Suggested Activities

1. Interview a school principal and/or a teacher about the potential for curriculum evaluation in their school. What is it exactly? When is it conducted? What are its uses? . . . benefits?
2. Collect six to ten definitions of curriculum evaluation from texts available and colleagues where you work. How do these differ in perspective and function?
3. Extend your understanding of curriculum development by further study about the deductive and the inductive approach.
4. Collect and read state department documents and accrediting agency guidelines which describe policy and standards for curriculum and evaluation in schools (See especially Appendix C).

Self-Assessment

Having completed this chapter:

1. Can you define in your own words curriculum evaluation as meaning making?
2. Can you summarize the general steps of the Tyler rationale for curriculum development?
3. Can you summarize the general steps of the curriculum development procedure proposed by Taba?
4. Can you suggest why curriculum evaluation is generally not done in schools?
5. Can you list four functions of evaluation?
6. Can you summarize the author's viewpoint on six curriculum evaluation principles?

References

Banathy, Bela. *Instructional Systems.* Belmont, California: Fearon Publishers, 1972.

Brubaker, Dale L. *Curriculum Planning: The Dynamics of Theory and Practice.* Glenview, Illinois: Scott, Foresman, 1982.

Cuban, Larry. Effective Schools: A Friendly But Cautionary Note. *Kappan,* Vol. 64, No. 10, June 1983, p. 695.

Curran, Edward A. N I E: An Agenda for the 80s. *Educational Researcher* Vol. 11, No. 5, May 1982, p. 11.

Edmonds, Ronald R. Programs of School Improvement: An Overview. *Educational Leadership* Vol 40, No. 3, December 1982, p. 4.

Goodlad, John I. *The Dynamics of Educational Change: Toward Responsive Schools.* New York: McGraw-Hill, 1975.

Klausmeier, Herbert. A Research Strategy for Educational Improvement. *Educational Researcher* Vol. 11, No. 2, February 1982, p. 10.

Mackenzie, Donald E. Research for School Improvement: An Appraisal of Some Recent Trends. *Educational Researcher* Vol. 12, No. 4, April 1983, p. 7.

National Commission on Excellence in Education. A Nation At Risk: The Imperative for Educational Reform. Washington, D.C., Department of Education, April 26, 1983.

Oliva, Peter F. *Developing the Curriculum.* Boston, Little, Brown, 1982.

Popham, W. James, and Eva Baker. *Systematic Instruction.* Englewood Cliffs, New Jersey: Prentice-Hall, 1970.

Raywid, Mary Anne. Schools of Choice: Their Current Nature and Prospects. *Kappan* Vol. 64, No. 10, p. 684.

Retsinas, Joan. Teachers and Professional Autonomy. *The Educational Forum* Vol. 47, No. 1, Fall 1982, p. 25.

Salmon-Cox, Leslie. Teachers and Standardized Achievement Tests: What's Really Happening? *Kappan* Vol. 62, No. 9, May 1981, p. 631.

Shine, William A., and Norma Goldman. Governance by Testing in New Jersey. *Educational Leadership* Vol. 38, No. 3, December 1980, p. 197.

Sproull, Lee, and David Zubrow. Standardized Testing from the Administrative Perspective. *Kappan* Vol. 62, No. 9, May 1981, p. 628.

Taba, Hilda. *Curriculum Development: Theory and Practice.* New York: Harcourt, Brace, and Javanovich, 1962.

Tyler, Ralph W. *Basic Principles of Curriculum and Instruction.* Chicago: University of Chicago Press, 1949.

Unruh, Glenys G. *Responsive Curriculum Development: Theory and Action.* Berkeley, California: McCutcheon, 1975.

Chapter 2

CURRICULUM PERSPECTIVES:
VIEWPOINTS FOR THE CURRICULUM EVALUATOR

As a result of this chapter, the reader should be able to:

1. Recognize and classify any school activity as either a part of the:
   b. formal curriculum
   b. instructional curriculum, or
   c. experiential curriculum
2. Recognize and discuss the relationships of the learner's experience events, the curriculum materials and resources, the instructional strategies and methods, and the curricular design, philosophy, and goals in planning, implementing, and evaluating the curriculum of the school.
3. Identify the priority and emphasis of the school activities in classroom instruction, curricular materials, staff development, and subject areas, to promote the four curriculum designs of: (1) academic skills; (2) inquiry and problem solving skills; (3) learner development, readiness, and remediation; and (4) self and social understanding.

"Back in the Middle West, of a Sunday afternoon, a lot of farmers used to walk around with their hands in their pockets and do an hour or two of what they called 'Sunday farming'. They didn't work very hard at it—you weren't supposed to work on Sunday. They just looked over the way things were going and sized up the problems and the jobs they had on their hands. But it was also their time to dream a little about the way things might be and to cherish their hopes for the future. Over time, out of some combination of tough-minded size-up and optimistic vision, they shaped up a plan of action."

from *Evaluation as Feedback and Guide*

An educator responsible for planning, implementing, and evaluating curriculum must have a walking-around-type viewer for seeing and understanding the action and activity of the school. Such a viewer must be portable and simple enough to carry "behind-the-eyes," in short, a curriculum perspective. The perspective needs to be useful for seeing and understanding such varied things as individual learners, instructional behaviors, curricular materials, subject matter fields, staff inservice needs, and school philosophy and organization to name but a few. Such a perspective has to remain simple enough to be remembered, but open enough to change and develop with changing situations and growing understanding and skill of the educator. This is the first essential perspective which an educator will need to be an effective curriculum evaluator.

Curriculum and curriculum development discussed in educational literature seem too complex to permit a portable, rememberable perspective for viewing the action of a school. This may be one reason why entire books on curriculum relegate one chapter to curriculum evaluation. In such a chapter the authors usually tell us that curriculum evaluation is important, it should be done, and then review one or two general evaluation models of other authors, and close the chapter. This seeming complexity of the notions about curriculum may also lead writers in the evaluation field to avoid curriculum issues altogether, and speak of the subject as program evaluation. We have set about a large task in this chapter to be clear, inclusive, and brief. For this undertaking, three ideas have been gleaned from the study of curriculum which in their essence can be remembered, are open enough to use in almost all areas of schooling, and can be developed in detail, depending on the needs of a specific situation.

CURRICULUM EXISTS IN LEVELS

The idea of curriculum levels can be attributed to John Goodlad (1983) in the major research effort known as, A Study of Schooling. Curriculum levels are the different planes within which the curriculum of a school may be found. Goodlad suggested that five such levels may exist. Though we will examine all of these, three of these curriculum levels seem most practical.

Ideal Curriculum Level

This is a conceptual description of a curriculum or program which suggests how the curriculum would work ideally. It may be a written description or perhaps a film portrayal of how the program is supposed to work in an utopian sense. From this ideal representation of the program or curriculum, we may learn about its philosophical position, the view of what the model learner is like, the concept of human development, and the position in learning psychology taken by the authors of the program. The advantages of examining the ideal curriculum as described in literature or portrayed in film vignettes are the opportunity of matching school philosophy and learning priorities and school and community culture with the tenets of the curriculum.

An example of such an ideal curriculum level may be the original ten-page article by Jerome Bruner (1967) called, Man: A Course of Study. In this article Bruner clearly sets forth a relativist philosophy of culture and describes the process approach by which learners might understand what makes man human, how did man get that way, and how we could become more human (Bruner's use of the term man was used to describe humankind and preceded, in any case, the era of critical attention to nonsexist language). The practical teaching of such a curriculum is only described. Had educators critically examined the precepts of this description of an ideal level of a 5th grade social studies curriculum, they might have considered their relationship to the students, school, and community before jumping on a curriculum bandwagon.

Goodlad and his researchers eventually discarded the ideal level of the curriculum from their research into schooling, commenting that such a level may not actually exist in schools. And, indeed, it does not. It exists in a description of concepts and may have little value except in the initial stages of selecting a curricular program.

Formal Curriculum Level

Formal curriculum refers to the written documents which describe the curriculum. If a school principal should hand you a notebook titled Mathematics Curriculum Guide or Mathematics Course of Study, this would represent the formal level of the mathematics curriculum. When teachers say they worked as a committee and developed a curriculum, they usually mean a document, a formal level of the curriculum. Many definitions of curriculum refer to the planned course of study to be taught. The formal level of curriculum also refers to written documents about state mandated standards, school philosophy statements, and other written statements of policy adopted by boards of education as well as lesson plans and teacher guides used in planning.

Instructional Curriculum Level

The teacher in the classroom has a perception of what the curriculum is and should be. This is the instructional level of the curriculum. The personal philosophy, knowledge, priorities, and style of the teacher strongly influence what is taught behind the classroom door. It is also evident to every experienced classroom teacher that the classroom activity and situation itself require almost constant decision making by the teacher. It may be that a teacher makes as many as three hundred micro-decisions per hour while engaged in classroom teaching. This curriculum as perceived by the teacher is referred to as the instructional curriculum level. An appropriate curriculum definition for this level could be "what is taught in the school."

To expect that what is in the curriculum guide, the formal level of curriculum, is what should be and is going on in the classroom in some identical one-for-one replacement notion is an utterly simplistic idea, perhaps even an unprofessional view of teachers, and almost certainly an impossibility to achieve with any relevance for the learners.

Curriculum mapping, a procedure promoted by Fenwick English (1980) to record what the curriculum is like as teachers teach it, is an attempt to bring the formal curriculum into line with the instructional curriculum. The procedure also presumes that curriculum development and improvement would more realistically start with what the teachers are doing.

Experiential Curriculum Level

The experiential curriculum is that curriculum perceived and experienced by the learner. It is apparent that learning itself is an individual happening which is influenced by the learner's background, previous learning, motivations, purpose, and interest to name a few such conditions. The experiential level of curriculum identifies a kind of curriculum which is really the result or the outcome of all the activities of schooling. The value of understanding the experiential level curriculum is related to how relevant the curriculum is and what needs the learners have.

It is very simplistic to assume that learners interpret, understand, and gain skill in exactly the way the teacher intended or the formal curriculum described. One example of this relationship was suggested by a study of learning objectives. Having interviewed the teacher about the learning objectives for several activities, the learners were asked what they were doing and why they were doing it. Some described a purpose for the activity much like the teacher's, some had no purpose which they could describe, and one group described very individual and insightful reasons for their activity which were certainly significant and yet not like the explanation which the teacher had provided. Those who would seek congruence in the curriculum levels might be more interested in ways for all learners to perceive a purpose more like the teacher's. Those persons concerned with personal relevance and meaning for the activities of school might be interested in how all learners could behave like the third group in the study. A more complete perspective might be to encourage both viewpoints from each learner. In either case the experiential curriculum level is a valuable perspective and is often ignored in the development and improvement of curriculum.

Operational Curriculum Level

The operational curriculum level was suggested by Goodlad to be that view of the curriculum which can be seen and described by an outside person not directly involved in the leadership, teaching, or learning of the school. Such a perspective may provide insights about the school program of which participants are unaware.

This perspective is especially helpful in bringing to light the out-of-awareness part of the curriculum. Sometimes the assumption behind the way things are done in school has been lost to the leadership and the teachers. For instance, a school program which separated children by grade level in every school activity was followed at one school. The principal and faculty revealed that their procedures were the only way to cope with the "natural" tendency of older children to intimidate and perhaps endanger younger children. It took an outside observer to help the staff examine the school procedures which were reinforcing and making this behavior come true. It was a learned response instead of a natural character of the school children.

The value of the idea of curriculum levels for a developer or evaluator lies in being able to look at apparent inconsistencies in the program and to understand and communicate from different points of view. For example, a supervisor may take a great deal of ownership in the paper document called the curriculum guide. The teacher, on the other hand, may view the guide as an imposition on what are the real needs and issues of learners in the classroom. Further, the learners may follow routines of schooling for years and rarely use the objectives or activities of lessons to develop their own personal meanings.

The most important of these five levels for the curriculum worker are likely the formal, the instructional, and the experiential. These three identify the very practical events of curriculum in schools. They help to isolate the issues and the inconsistencies in what goes on in the school curriculum. They suggest where the problems can be dealt with and what levels may not be getting attention. Curriculum workers can use the concept of levels as one of the helpful ideas for maintaining a perspective about curriculum evaluation.

THE CURRICULUM WHEEL

The second of these idea perspectives about curriculum which can be used as a mental organizer and viewer of school activities is called the Curriculum Wheel. It is simply a diagram which puts into relationship the continuous process of planning, implementing, and outcomes with the five most important components of a school learning program: the curricular design, the instructional means, the resources, the staff development, and the learner experience cycle. Figure 1 represents the processes and components in an easily remembered diagram. The outer edge of the wheel suggests the continuous and circular processes of planning, implementing, and outcomes. The hub of the wheel also turning through planning, implementing, and outcomes processes is the experience cycle of the learner. This experience cycle occurs in a series of events or personal learning activities involving: (1) awareness and focus of the learner (a part of the planning end of the learning loop); (2) acquiring, practicing, interacting (a middle phase of the learning loop akin to implementing) and (3) adapting, performing, internalizing (a phase of the learning loop akin to outcomes). This learner experience cycle repeats through event after event in each class, subject, and activity. The experience cycle is influenced by the resources or things and materials available to the learner, by the instructor's means and her/his style of influence and intervention as a significant actor in the learner's experience. The experience cycle is influenced by the assumptions, values, and biases of the curriculum design such as whether we value accuracy of performance in the curriculum or trial and error or invention and problem solving. Finally, the experience cycle of the learner is indirectly influenced by the support and development of professional skill of the teachers through the staff development component of the program.

Figure 1
Curriculum Domain

We could likewise take any other component of the curriculum wheel such as instructional means and illustrate how it goes through a planning, implementing, and outcomes cycle, and how the other components, curriculum design, resources, staff development and learner experience cycle, influence it.

These five components are not discrete, bounded entities in the school program. In a systems view, these five components transact and mutually influence each other. All five components and the continuous processes are represented within each individual component as well as exist as parts of a total curriculum system.

The value of such a perspective for the curriculum worker is in the realization that affecting any part of the curriculum wheel of components and processes will have consequences for other parts of the curriculum system.

The most dramatic example of unawareness of this holistic nature of curriculum was told of a superintendent many years ago in a state far, far away. It seems he got enthused over an innovation in those years called Modern Math while at an administrators' conference. On returning home he got a committee of teachers together to order one of the several text series then available. A month or so after the textbooks had arrived and been distributed, he noticed that the teachers were using the old books in classes. So on a Saturday the superintendent and custodian removed all the old books from classrooms and took them to the incinerator. Such an anecdote is from another age and place and probably belongs in a joke book about superintendents, but it does remind us vividly of the lack of perspective of all the components in the curriculum system of the diagram.

The idea of the curriculum wheel is easy to remember and communicate. It can be imagined or diagrammed, for example, during a faculty meeting and elaborated as the situation requires to suggest ways in which curriculum, instruction, learning, materials and resources, and staff development are involved and related in any schooling issue, topic, or discipline.

A FOUR-PHASE CURRICULUM DESIGN

A third perspective which can be remembered and used to understand and communicate about the curriculum is that all curricula have four phases to their design. Every curriculum design gives some attention to: (1) self development and social understanding; (2) the readiness and remediation of a developmental curriculum; (3) the acquisition of the basic skills of the culture we live in and the academic disciplines; and (4) inquiry, problem solving, and reasoning.

These four phases of a curriculum design are individually compatible with different educational philosophies and consequently different learning theories (Eisner and Valence, 1974). The four phases are at odds with each other in some practical and methodological ways. For example, the humanist tradition often follows a phenomenological learning and teaching psychology in developing self and social understanding, while the acquisition of skills and knowledge design usually follows the essentialist philosophical tradition and learning (McNeil, 1981). The process-product issue is basic to the difference between learning as inquiry and learning as acquisition of knowledge.

The implication of these differences in curriculum designs and philosophical arguments seems to be that we must choose one and omit the others. But the practical matter is that we must include, not choose. These educational ends and value positions are all good, and each describes the development of a learner and a learning process which ought to be pursued. Each has benefits and each suggests contradictions with the other phases. In fact, almost all school philosophy statements refer to each of these curricular outcomes, but seldom does a school curriculum include a conscientious and practical and balanced effort in pursuit of all these ends.

The four phases of curriculum design are seldom dealt with together in the curriculum. For the most part inquiry and independent decision making are phrases included in a philosophy statement, but not a planned state of the teaching and learning program. Readiness and remediation are almost never referred to in a philosophy statement of a school. Many teachers look on remediation needs as some slightly embarrassing lack of normalcy in some students. A curriculum effort for readiness and remediation is usually a combination of summer school make-up classes and/or repeating the year at grade level. The self and social understanding curriculum too often refers to extracurricular activities of the school, a positive discipline code, student government activities for a few, and some career counseling by the guidance department. The practical priority for most schools is the acquisition of academic knowledge through a curriculum categorized by subject areas. This priority is, no doubt, correct, but the four phases of a complete curriculum design can and should be included in every school curriculum, in each discipline area, in every unit of study, and most importantly in every learner's set of experiences with each curriculum.

SPECIFICS OF THE FOUR PHASES OF CURRICULUM DESIGN

The idea of four phases of an inclusive curriculum design can be developed in great detail. In Table 1 the nature of the learner which is envisioned in each of these four phases is suggested. It is apparent that the analogy of the learner in each phase is a different and valuable view of human nature.

Table 1
A Four Phase Curriculum Design Concept of the Learner

	PROBLEM SOLVING	BASIC SKILLS	READINESS	SELF UNDERSTANDING
LEARNER	to continue to learn; to face the unknown	tools to live by; tools of the culture	to reach entry; stages of growth, maturity skills	to know oneself and one's talents to be productive to live and work with others

In Table 2 we add the learning processes which might be compatible with each of the phases and consistent with the first category of the learner. It can now be seen that the different designs raise conflicts. For example, in the problem solving/inquiry process of learning we must have trials and mistakes and new trials. In the learning process associated with basic and academic skills and knowledge, we seek practice activities for accuracy. Errors in spelling, for example, cannot be tolerated. Errors in problem solving are not only acceptable, but are necessary to make progress.

Table 3 elaborates the four phases of a complete curriculum design as it might show the choices and the conflicts between the four. This chart shows only an example of how each phase might be designed, not the only way it could or should be spelled out. The chart presented at this point merely shows that the four phases of a complete curriculum design are not just an interesting philosophical argument. Such an approach can be clearly spelled out in such components as what types of learner motivation to build upon, compatible instructional methods, classroom control approach, and how evaluation of learning might take place. The chart is but an example. The reader should mentally fold up the chart until only the names of four phases of a complete curriculum design remain. These four ideas of a total curriculum design can be used as a viewpoint for understanding the priority expressed in the curriculum guides and philosophy of a school, in what is taught and how, in what learners are experiencing, in the

Table 2
A Four Phase Curriculum Design
The Learner and Learning Process

	PROBLEM SOLVING	BASIC SKILLS	READINESS	SELF UNDERSTANDING
LEARNER	to continue to learn; to face the unknown	tools to live by; tools of the culture	to reach entry; stages of growth, maturity skills	to know yourself and your talents to be productive
LEARNING PROCESS	trial and error; insights; concept formation; research skills	repetition practice; overlearning; applications	exploratory mastery; refresh/ relearn	self-knowing; affective; developmental; imitative

curriculum materials, the school organization, and the staff development support.

PUTTING A CURRICULUM PERSPECTIVE TO WORK

Peters and Waterman in *In Search of Excellence* refer to remembered frameworks attained through knowledge and experience as vocabularies of patterns. The number of these vocabularies of patterns remembered and recognized differs according to the knowledge background and expertise level of individuals. It was suggested in the same book that good chess players may recognize some 2000 patterns on the game board, while a chess master may have a recognition vocabulary of perhaps 50,000 game board patterns. Like a chess master, a curriculum developer and evaluator needs the knowledge and expertise to see and recognize the patterns of curriculum, instruction, and learning in action. The three perspectives described here (curriculum levels, the curriculum wheel, and the four-phase curriculum design) are mental perspectives which help the curriculum evaluator look for expected patterns in the school program and help recognize unexpected patterns.

The use of mental perspectives by the curriculum evaluator is analogous to the pattern recognition of the chess master. The chess master recognizes much earlier in the game what the pattern is, what alternatives may be coming, what options are available, what mistakes may be

Table 3
A Four Phase Curriculum Design

	PROBLEM SOLVING	BASIC SKILLS	READINESS	SELF UNDERSTANDING
LEARNER	to continue to learn; to face the unknown	tools to live by; tools of the culture	to reach entry; stages of growth, maturity skills	to know yourself and your talents to be productive
LEARNING PROCESS	trial and error; insights; concept formation; research skills	repetition practice; overlearning; applications	exploratory mastery; refresh/ relearn	self-knowing; affective; developmental; imitative
CONTENT OR KNOWLEDGE FORM	inter-disciplinary	specific discipline linear sequence of steps	pre-content areas of knowledge	expressive and fine arts; human development value clarification hobbies/ vocational interests
MOTIVATION	HI-internal search closure LO-external peers outcomes	HI-external rewards for achieve-ment, com-petition LO-internal skill repertoire self-confidence	HI-internal LO-external	HI-internal actualization interests LO-external peers relatedness
INSTRUCTIONAL METHODS	task/research groups facilitating identifying resouces	drill didactic flashcards quizzes learning packets	diagnosis/ assessment concrete activity games/play	counseling/ advising small groups individual projects apprenticeships life planning
TEACHER CONTROL STRUCTURE	LO	HI	HI/LO	LO
EVALUATION FORMS	project evidence by self and group	performance testing; written and oral testing by self and teacher	proficiency testing performance testing by observa-tion/teacher	self understanding and actualization by self

avoided, what assumptions or hypotheses to check out further. The curriculum evaluator, keeping in mind these and other self-constructed perspectives, should be able to visit a school, talk with the principal, interact with teachers, observe facilities, see traffic patterns and materials displays, and in a short time form some tentative ideas about the kind of curriculum and its phases which are described, taught, and experienced in the school. Such ideas need to be constantly modified and confirmed throughout the procedures of curriculum development and evaluation, but they are clearly useful. The chess master and the curriculum evaluator analogy is useful but limited. In chess the moves are two dimensional and limited to a recreational win or lose conflict between two individuals. In the schooling setting the purposes, conditions, individuals are much more complex, subtle, and real.

The curriculum evaluator might use perspectives to understand first impressions of a school, to sort out differences of opinion, apparent inconsistencies, to recognize the effect of one part of a curriculum upon other parts. Perspectives help with early recognition, apparent inconsistencies, making options clear, avoiding past mistakes, and noting new possibilities and options.

SUMMARY

Curriculum, instruction, and learning must be viewed and understood in total perspective if we are to improve schools through evaluation. We must have frameworks which help us to understand the influences of all components of the school. This chapter offers three such frameworks or perspectives. Levels of curriculum have been defined and exemplified. This is a very helpful step in sorting out different interpretations about the curriculum. Goodlad has suggested ideal level, formal (document) level of the curriculum, instructional level (what the teacher perceives), experiential level (what the learner perceives), and operational level of the curriculum.

A second perspective or framework for understanding the curriculum of the school is called the curriculum wheel. This is an attempt to illustrate the interacting and influencing nature of curriculum design, instructional program, learner experience, curriculum resources, and staff development in the planning, implementing, and evaluating of curriculum.

The third perspective described is the curriculum design of four phases. The proposal explained here is that every learner, lesson, classroom, course, or program can be examined for its design and method to promote inquiry, achievement skills, readiness, and self and social development.

These perspectives offer the educator frames of orientation to understand the intentions, processes, and outcomes of the curriculum of the school. They are helpful in seeing connections, understanding behavior, and making sense of the complex and profuse reality of the school situation.

Suggested Activities

1. Diagram and write an explanation of a curriculum perspective which you have acquired from experience and practice, and which helps you understand teaching and learning in a school or classroom.
2. Using the four phases curriculum design framework, observe a school or classroom with one other person. Share your insights about the priorities and design of the teaching-learning situation.
3. Interview an evaluation specialist from a large school district and find out what perspectives or mental framework he/she uses to initially understand a teaching/learning program.
4. Search the curriculum literature to identify additional curriculum frameworks which might be useful for a curriculum evaluator to add to his/her "vocabulary of perspectives."
5. Investigate the contrast and similarity of the instructional vs. the experiential curriculum levels by finding out the purpose and strategies which a teacher has for a lesson and conversing with some of the students during or after the lesson about the purpose and meaning which they perceive about the lesson.

Self-Assessment

Having completed this chapter:

1. Can you give examples and classify school events according to these levels: formal curriculum, instructional curriculum, experiential curriculum?
2. Can you describe the relationship of curriculum design, instructional method, learning resources, staff development, and experience events of the learner?
3. Can you recognize the priority and balance of the curriculum in any classroom you visit for inquiry learning, academic skills, readiness and remediation, and self development and social learning?

Bibliography

Bruner, Jerome. *Toward a Theory of Instruction.* Cambridge, Mass.: Belknap Press, 1967.

English, Fenwick W. "Curriculum Mapping." *Educational Leadership.* Vol. 37, No. 7, April 1980, p. 558

Goodlad, John *A Place Called School.* New York: McGraw-Hill, 1983.

Peters, Thomas J. and Waterman, Robert H. *In Search of Excellence.* New York: Harper and Row, 1982.

Wilhelms, Fred T. (ed). *Evaluation as Feedback and Guide.* Washington, D.C.: Association for Supervision and Curriculum Development, 1967.

Eisner, Elliot W., and Elizabeth Valence. *Conflicting Conceptions of Curriculum.* Berkeley, Calif.: McCutchan, 1973.

McNeil, John D. *Curriculum: A Comprehensive Introduction* (2nd Ed.). Boston: Little, Brown, 1981.

Chapter 3

FEEDBACK:
THE SEARCH FOR VALUABLE INFORMATION

As a result of this chapter, the reader should be able to:

1. Define and amplify the concept of feedback.
2. List nine guidelines which relate to the giving and receiving of feedback.
3. Critique four traditional models of evaluation using the expanded definition and guidelines related to feedback.
4. Suggest some specific characteristics of an evaluation plan which can be judged on the basis of the concept of feedback.

"We see things not as they are, but as we are." From *A Course in Miracles.*

Bats are able to fly through experimental mazes in total darkness without any accident or difficulty. They send out high pitched sound waves which bounce off the objects around them. These reflected sounds are heard and interpreted with incredible speed and accuracy. So bats can "see" by listening to responses from messages which they have sent (Jung, 1972, p. 109). These returning messages are called feedback.

We humans, too, make our way in our daily lives by means of feedback. The child learning to walk and the adult getting ready for an important appointment both are operating on the principle of feedback. The nerve endings in the child's feet and in the inner ear transmit information for physical and muscular adjustment. The adult looks in the mirror to get information for hair combing, cleanliness, and self-assurance. Such a process is a built-in characteristic of a living system.

A DEFINITION OF FEEDBACK

Feedback is sought information which has the potential to influence behavior, meaning, and growth. This definition is simple and condensed, yet it attends to the entire study of evaluation. Such a definition needs a brief amplification of its component parts to show how it represents so much with such an economy of words.

First, feedback *is sought information.* We are not just reactors to an environment around us. We have intentions and choice. We are seekers of the information we need to fulfill our intentions and our goals. "How do I get to Carnegie Hall?" as the old joke goes. Feedback is sought information.

This first phase of the definition also tells us something about nonfeedback, what feedback is not. Information presented to you which you did not seek is not feedback. It may be true, it may be supportive, it may be critical, but it is not feedback. When a person says, "Let me give you a piece of advice," it is well to remember that you do have a choice. You may seek this out, you may personally give to this advice the status of feedback, or you may not. Only the receiver can decide what status information or opinion has.

Second, feedback is sought information *which has the potential* . . . for information to have potential as feedback it must fit the context of the situation and the intention. It also must be significant as opposed to insignificant information, and it must be accurate and not faulty. Information fits the context of our situation to greater or lesser degree. So, for example, the experimental psychologist can report to us on reinforcement and behavior of rats and pigeons. Does it fit the context of a classroom of learners? (I am acquainted with a superior teacher who got great insight into classroom management from just such experimental work.)

Does the information fit our intention? In this case we are not only concerned with our purpose or goal, but what we value. In the example above, of rats and pigeons, our disciplined classroom environment may be the goal, but we may greatly value choice and self-discipline in the learner. We may, therefore, decide that this information about experiments with reinforcement does not fit; it does not have potential for us.

Overwhelming amounts of information can be generated and sorted out from the world around us. We cannot possibly cope with all that could be available. So we must decide what to get and use. The bat has no difficulty recognizing its own reflected sound among other background noises. We must choose to get information which is the most useful. We must ignore information which, like the background noise, cannot be used for our context and purpose. Likewise, the information must be accurate and not faulty. For example, three phone calls from irate parents to the school principal in a single morning may be very persuasive, yet not represent the school community accurately.

Third, feedback is sought information which has the potential *to influence* . . . feedback which one seeks will only have influence if one is ready to receive it, does, in fact, receive it, does understand and believe it, and is *able* to and *will* respond. If the bat, for instance, did not get the information it sought, the result would be a crash landing sooner or later. Information provided too late for a moment of decision or provided for a decision which is already made will have no influence. Information which cannot be understood or believed will not have influence. For example, a new invention called radar was apparently working on the morning of December 7, 1941, in Hawaii, but it had no influence on the events which did follow. In one case, that fateful morning, it was not received; in another case it was not believed, and finally, there was no system or organization available which could or would respond.

In the last criteria, "unable to respond," one may get information about things which cannot be changed. For example, a criterion of physical height may be a requirement to which a person cannot respond.

Last, feedback is sought information which has the potential to influence *behavior, meaning, and growth.* Behavior, here, means simply things we are able to do. Feedback may influence us to maintain our behavior as it is, to change our behavior a little, or to change our behavior a great deal.

Meaning is our intellectual understanding and valuing, our perspective of our world. Meaning also can be influenced by feedback in the gradations of change, a minor change, a large change, or no change at all. Growth is perhaps the integration of behavior and meaning in a new state of development. It may also be subject to the same gradations of change.

GUIDELINES FOR SEEKING/ACCEPTING FEEDBACK

The following guidelines are based upon the definition of feedback and are general rules of thumb which are useful in many situation. They have been adapted from the process of giving and receiving feedback in interpersonal communications (Jung, 1972, p. 112) but are now selected and reformed to address feedback use in general.

1. STATE WHAT YOU WANT FEEDBACK ABOUT
   Seek feedback about specific things, make your needs clear, your question specific.
2. APPROPRIATE READINESS FOR FEEDBACK
   The people involved must be attentive to the information.
3. APPROPRIATE TIMES AND PLACES
   Feedback too late or too early will never be used. Feedback provided for dramatic effect in a public forum may serve other agenda than influence of behavior, meaning and growth.
4. FEEDBACK IS MEANT TO BE HELPFUL
   Watch out for other agenda for seeking/accepting feedback.
5. FEEDBACK IS DESCRIPTIVE, NOT INTERPRETIVE
   The meanings of information provided must be developed by the receivers.
6. CHANGE MUST BE POSSIBLE
   Changeable things should be addressed with the choice for change under the receiver's control.
7. CHOICE FOR CHANGE
   Feedback should never be presented so as to demand a change or a certain outcome.
8. FEEDBACK SHOULD NOT OVERLOAD
   Too much information can be overwhelming. Sift it out and address only the need or goal that was stated.
9. FEEDBACK SHOULD BE SPECIFIC
   Generalities are often vague and can be interpreted in many ways. Be specific and focused in providing feedback.

EVALUATION MODELS AND THE CONCEPT OF FEEDBACK

The concept of feedback describes a natural process which occurs in all living systems and has the potential to influence behavior, meaning, and growth. There are several generic models of evaluation in the field of education. How faithfully the guidelines for feedback can be followed in each of these evaluation models determines in part what the advantages and disadvantages are and what dilemmas must be faced in using each model.

Model I: Evaluation as Measurement

"A well-organized coordinated testing program can provide a lot of answers for a lot of people." This is the kind of statement which suggests a view of *Evaluation as Measurement* (Stufflebeam, 1971). Some schools have a standardized testing program for all pupils which consumes a week of school calendar each Spring, after which the tests are sent away for scoring. Individual, grade level, and school means are reported and recorded in individual student folders; sometimes school means are reported in the newspaper, and that is about the end of the process.

Based on the definition of feedback, we could agree that the information was sought at least as a school board or administrative policy. Whether the information was truly sought by the teacher is doubtful. Does the information influence behavior? The answer may be yes. In many cases teachers and school staffs increase their time at getting the learners ready for the test in hopes that their school will rank above the mean or their school will show "most improvement" in scores in one year. This change in behavior soon leads to the questions of accurate and believable information. As to whether this information influences meaning and growth, there may be doubt.

In review of the guidelines for feedback as a critique of the Evaluation as Measurement model, the guideline violations which appear most obvious are: Purpose of the feedback can easily be overlooked under generalities like, "It's good to know how we are doing," and other vagaries. Information is not specific and usually comes too late to relate to the learners who took the test. The information may not relate to the curriculum being taught or have influence upon its development. Authors like Fenwick English have attempted through curriculum management models to develop this relationship more systematically.

Model II: Objectives—Output Congruence Evaluation

From Tyler (Tyler, 1949, p. 104) we get a succinct definition of this model, " . . . evaluation is essentially the process of determining to what extent the educational objectives are actually being realized . . . in the behavior patterns of the student."

When we consider the feedback definition of this rather widely accepted model, we find that information is sought. Whether this measure of learner behavior against objectives can influence behavior, meaning and growth, depends upon what we know about how the learners were taught, and is based upon the assumption that specific behaviors tested are a complete and sufficient demonstration of an educational objective.

The limitations of this model as they relate to the guidelines for seeking/accepting feedback are appropriate timing to influence behavior and growth. The students are tested at the end of the program. Feedback is meant to be helpful, and choice and change must be possible. After the completion of the course it may be difficult to gain much insight into what to change or to improve upon.

Model III: Evaluation as Judgment

In this model, professionals render a judgment about the value of an educational program. The presented report of the professionals is the evaluation. This is often the mode used by accrediting agencies and blue ribbon panel committees.

This model only partially meets the conceptual criteria of feedback. It is very likely meant to influence change, but it may not be sought information by some members of the school staff.

The feedback guidelines in most jeopardy by this model are that it may not leave the interpretation of the evidence or the choice for change to the receiver of the feedback.

Model IV: Information for Decision Making

In the Decision Making Model, evaluation is defined as the science of providing information for decision making (Stufflebeam, 1971). This model seems to meet most of the conceptual criteria of feedback, sought information for a specific purpose with choice about change to be made based upon the information. The most troublesome of the feedback guidelines for this model seems to be that decision making is sometimes actually settled before information is sought. Thus, the timing of feedback and the value laden quality of some decision making sometimes limits the potential of this process to influence change.

The guidelines for seeking/accepting feedback are particularly helpful as a plan for evaluation is drawn up and implemented. As the plans and procedures of evaluation stray from the concept and guidelines of feedback, the plan and procedure itself become less and less like the natural process inherent in a living system. This moving away from a true feedback process means that the procedure itself becomes more artificial and less likely to influence change in behavior, meaning, and growth.

DEFINING EVALUATION AS FEEDBACK

It would be appropriate to develop a definition of evaluation in education which holds to the conceptual nature of feedback and can also accommodate the positive aspects of these alternate models of evaluation. Lucille Jordan offers a definition which may meet these qualifications in the foreword of the publication, *Applied Strategies for Curriculum Evaluation.* She says, "Evaluation is the process of making meaning out of experience and converting experience into meaningful behavior, which results in better learning programs."

Evaluating Evaluations

Feedback as a concept can also provide a basis for the evaluation of the evaluation plan itself, the metaevaluation. The Evaluation Research Society (1981) identified 30 standards for program evaluation (see Appendix C). Several standards are very compatible with the concept of feedback as discussed here. For example, standard A1 recommends that those involved or affected by an evaluation should be identified so that their need can be addressed. Each of these stated standards should be critiqued using the feedback definition. It seems that for the evaluator a mental concept of the nature and definition of feedback would be a valuable framework for engaging in all aspects of an evaluation process.

SUMMARY

Feedback is sought information which has the potential to influence behavior, meaning, and growth. The first essential of feedback which gives information this potential is that the receiver of feedback is the one who initially seeks it out.

Several principles which guide the giving and receiving of feedback are useful in developing evaluation plans. These are: to state clearly what is wanted; to be ready and willing to attend to feedback. For giving feedback it must be: appropriate in time; given to be helpful; descriptive and not interpretive; a change must be possible; choice for change is left to the receiver; not too much at once; and focused on specifics. Of the four traditional evaluation models, each can be analyzed in terms of its congruence with principles of feedback. Evaluation as Measurement is actually a nonmodel and most likely to violate feedback guidelines. The other three models, Congruence, Judgment, and Decision Making, are each subject to strengths and limitations for fulfilling the concept of feedback. Specific evaluation plans and procedures can themselves be evaluated for quality and potential effectiveness by applying the definition and principles of feedback.

Suggested Activities

1. Obtain a copy of a plan for evaluation or an evaluation report from a school district near you. Analyze the plan or report for its relationship to the concept of feedback as presented in the chapter.
2. Interview a school manager or central office administrator about what essentials are necessary for an evaluation conducted in that school district. Identify from the interview which principles of effective feedback are expressed and valued and which ones, if any, are not.
3. Make a list of situations and events in which each of the following models of evaluation would be the most appropriate to follow:
   a. Objectives-Output Congruence Model
   b. Evaluation as Judgment Model
   c. Decision-Making Model
4. Search the evaluation literature for other models of evaluation. Critique these according to the definition and principles of feedback.
5. Study the Standards for Evaluation of Educational Programs (Appendix C). Determine which standards relate to the principles of feedback developed in this chapter.

Self-Assessment

Having completed the chapter:

1. Can you explain in detail and give examples of the concept of feedback?
2. What are useful guidelines for giving and receiving feedback?
3. Which of the traditional models of evaluation best incorporates the principles of the concept of feedback?
4. If you were asked to assess the quality of a curriculum evaluation plan, what criteria consistent with the concept of feedback would you use?

References

Brandt, Ronald, ed. *Applied Strategies for Curriculum Evaluation* Washington, D.C.: Association for Supervision and Curriculum Development, 1981.

Joint Committee on Standards for Educational Evaluation. *Standards For Evaluation of Educational Programs, Programs, and Materials.* New York: McGraw-Hill,

Jung, Charles, et al *Interpersonal Communications* Tuxedo, New York: Xicom, Inc., 1972.

Stufflebeam, Daniel L., et al *Education Evaluation and Decision Making* Phi Delta Kappa Study Committee on Evaluation Itasca, Illinois: F. E. Peacock Publishers, 1971.

Tyler, Ralph W. *Principles of Curriculum and Instruction* Chicago: University of Chicago Press, 1949.

Chapter 4

ISSUES IN CURRICULUM EVALUATION*

As a result of this chapter, the reader should be able to:

1. Identify issues in curriculum evaluation.
2. Analyze issues based on questions of purpose, setting, procedures, and meaning of the curriculum evaluation effort.
3. Construct practical responses to curriculum evaluation issues.

There are many issues to be dealt with when planning and conducting a curriculum evaluation (Stufflebeam, 1971). The conflict and consequences of these issues can be minimized if we are willing to first recognize them, second, clarify the issues with the people involved in the evaluation, and third, take some practical steps to limit the potentially harmful impact of each issue. The following is a list of some of the issues in the practical conduct of curriculum evaluation with a short discussion of some practical approaches for working through each issue.

ISSUE 1: EVALUATING TOO SOON

One of the pressing questions is, "When can we have proof that a curriculum works?" Board members and administrators, perhaps given the pressure of the day for accountability, behave as if a curriculum program should show learner achievement gains in one school year of use. That seems to be a reasonable request, but it probably is not. From what we now know about implementation steps, it is not reasonable to expect product outcomes of a comprehensive curriculum program to change in less than three years, and often longer. The consequence is that we evaluate for change in student outcomes in too short a time, and finding no change, we drop the program, or switch to another curriculum program and try that one for a year. At the end of a decade of such

*Reproduced by permission, NASSP Bulletin, February 1985

switches, the board, educators, public, editorial critics, and researchers can conclude that: (1) we should go back to the good oldfashioned way; (2) we are confusing everyone; and (3) we are wasting money. They also can wrongly conclude that the new curriculum programs do not work.

Our best response to the "When to evaluate" issue is to provide a clear three-to-five year plan for the implementation of the curriculum program, with a clear plan to provide evaluation feedback yearly about different aspects of the program, with student achievement outcomes to be measured at an appropriate stage.

ISSUE 2: IT NEVER HAPPENED

This issue of curriculum evaluation is related to the "Evaluating Too Soon" issue. In the former case we didn't wait long enough to look for effects. In many cases we evaluate something which, in fact, never happened. Charters and Jones (1973) refer to this as the "nonevent."

Charters and Jones were studying the effects of team teaching organizations in schools when they discovered that the program had often never been implemented. Evaluators may accept the program as a given if the users say they have adopted it. So there are many a modern math curriculum, or process science curriculum, or IGE school, or individualized reading program, or middle school, which may never have existed at all on the basis of its major objectives, concepts, and procedures.

The response to this issue has been to develop means to measure the presence of the program itself (Hall and Louks, 1977), the independent variable, at the same time we seek to measure the curriculum effects. Such measures examine the commitment of the administrators and teachers to the program, the resources, inservice and organizational procedures that were installed, classroom observations of changes in teaching behavior, and learner behavior which fit the program concepts.

ISSUE 3: COMPARING CURRICULA

If you were asked to evaluate two 1200-pound, brown, four-footed, hoofed, furry mammals on the basic criterion of running speed, that might sound reasonable. The two are indeed alike on some essentials, namely large and four-footed. But if you were told that one is a horse and one is a cow, you would immediately see that the creatures are different, and such a comparison is unfair to the cow. But measured on the criterion of milk-giving, it is unfair to the horse. Like the analogy of furry, brown mammals, we have compared curriculum programs like modern vs. traditional mathematics on computation speed and accuracy, and generally found that traditional mathematics is best. Usually we did not test learners on such things as thinking or conceptualizing using mathematics which would likely show that modern math was better.

Any two programs or methods in the same curriculum area, while they may look similar, will have some purposes which each serves uniquely and some purposes which overlap, which both programs or methods can serve. This must first be made clear to all persons involved in an evaluation, and then steps must be taken to evaluate for effects of the unique as well as the overlapping purposes.

ISSUE 4: NO SIGNIFICANT DIFFERENCE

Evaluation studies of curriculum programs may show no significant difference. Yet when the teachers and participants are interviewed, they are convinced of positive subtle and pervasive effects of the program. This is probably the issue which most leads professionals to declare that the most important effects of a program cannot be measured. The consequences of a no significant difference finding may seriously affect the support and resources of a program when in a less formal way the program shows considerable influence.

A curriculum evaluation effort must seek the true effects of a program by combining the gathering of hard and soft data. Hard data are composed of quantifiable information which can be collected by observation or instruments which are structured and objective. Hard data answer the questions, What?, How much? Soft data are the information of quality which attend to impressions, interpretation, and nuance. Soft data answer the question, "Why? Persons involved in an evaluation process must be helped to understand that the true and credible findings of a study can only be attained by seeking and paying attention to both kinds of data. The no significant difference conclusion may be only half answered.

A second reason why the *no significant difference* dilemma arises may be due to the nature of how programs affect different kinds of students. If all students are measured by the same means, the effects which differ with boys or girls, with differences in readiness, motivation, or learning style, may all be lost by looking at averages of all children by grade level or by school.

ISSUE 5: SKEPTICISM

When each explanation of a curriculum evaluation provided to a board or an administrator is met with a further question which begins, "Yes, but . . . ," you can be sure the program is being perceived with skepticism.

If a curriculum has a supportive political-influential environment, program reviewers such as board members or administrators will be accepting of all forms of feedback and reaction from rating surveys of the teachers to "So pleased . . . " letters from parents. When the political-influential climate has become skeptical, almost no information is quite acceptable.

Within a supportive environment, it is foresighted for program evaluators to record and file for the future all the fortuitous types of feedback which become available. Within a skeptical environment the evaluators would be wise to move to as rigorous an experimental-control design for the program as can be mustered. Experimental design may severely limit the assessment of complex and interacting variables, and may have a horse vs. cow comparison to the control group experience; but for all its limitations, it does have the charm of science, and the hardest skeptic will often accede to or support such an evaluation.

ISSUE 6: EVALUATING THE SOLUTION

Evaluation designs and plans should start with a clearly stated question. We must be sure the evaluation is a search for information to a problem and *not just supportive rationale for a solution which certain people already have in mind.* The following question, "How can we get teachers to stop lecturing so much?" is a solution question (Kinghorn, 1974). It contains the outcome we seek. Such questions can be very threatening to teachers and others. They are demands for change which are hidden in an evaluation procedure. A principle of feedback is being violated, namely, that choice and change are ultimately the domain of the receiver of feedback. Evaluation cannot be an answer going in search of support.

A problem question in the same topic category might have been, "How much do teachers lecture?" or, "What are the most effective uses of lecture?"

A practical approach here is to avoid solution questions for the most part. If you have a solution question, make very clear to all participants that the agenda could be dealt with on other grounds than an evaluation procedure.

ISSUE 7: WHAT ARE WE REALLY MEASURING?

SAT scores by school averages (neighborhood schools) were once correlated with the number of registered voters in the precinct of each school in a large city district. With two exceptions in more than sixty schools the SAT scores ranked high to low exactly like the voter registration.

Evaluating curriculum is not a procedure of administering a well known test and then pronouncing schools above the mean as good. The test in the example above may have been measuring things about the educational program of each school. But it was surely measuring some other socioeconomic factors as well.

Measuring is not evaluating; and testing every pupil, by itself, is not a means to judge curriculum programs. This sort of obvious statement may not be grasped by some involved in the educational program. There are other things which can be done. There should be a good reason why a test is selected and why thousands of hours of pupil learning time are devoted to taking it. Failing a clear response to why use a particular test, the curriculum evaluator can item analyze the test to determine which test items relate to the curriculum and which do not. The evaluator can further list the objectives and topics of the curriculum which are not addressed by the test. The testing center can usually supply scores by item for a standardized test requested or a hand scoring of relevant items can be conducted before the tests are sent away.

ISSUE 8: INSIDE AND OUTSIDE

Persons within a curriculum program tend to evaluate a program favorably. Persons from outside a curriculum program who evaluate it tend to be less favorable. The further the evaluator is from the program, the more critical seem to be the conclusions. As an example, read the articles on education from the local school district newsletter, the daily newspaper of the area, and the education section of a nationally published weekly magazine. The more general, the more removed from the specific program the evaluation is, the more critical it is.

The balance is attempted, for example, in accreditation evaluations where an internal self-study is conducted and a visiting committee comes from outside the program. It seems that neither the inside nor the outside can be valid alone. When a skeptical political environment is pervasive, the board would perhaps favor an outside evaluator. It is essential to attend to both the inside and the outside view for a better attempt at validity.

ISSUE 9: SOMETHING IS WRONG

Sometimes programs don't get evaluated unless there is a problem; something is going wrong and there may be a need to find out who is at fault. Evaluation is too often equated with "something is going wrong." Evaluation by its very process may be negative because it is set up to find the gaps, the discrepancies, the breaks, the needs, and deficits.

It is recommended that evaluation be based upon feedback principles as a continuing search for meaning, a part of regular and ongoing program development, not some back-burner procedure that is brought into operation when problem symptoms arise.

ISSUE 10: THE HIDDEN MEANINGS

When the International Association for the Evaluation of Educational Achievement reported its findings on reading comprehension of seventeen year olds in 22 countries, the United States ranked 12th (Sava, 1975), a mediocre showing indeed. Finally, it was noticed that 75% of all U.S. young people of seventeen years are in school and were represented in the sample. In other countries, only an elite of students are still in school at 17 years of age, and are represented in the sample. Partitioning the U.S. sample for the top elite of the seventeen-year-old population resulted in a change of rank from 12th place to 1st place among the nations.

The example holds for any level of curriculum evaluation; you don't just report it, you must understand it and note the several meanings which evaluation findings may have.

ISSUE 11: VALIDATING BY PUBLISHING

"If it's in the Sun, it must be so," said little Virginia's father about fifty years ago when she asked about Santa Claus. What becomes published about a program or a school gains a credibility by out-competing any other presentation or opinion and reinforcing itself by cyclic communication throughout the community.

Such information is often published because the writer has found a clever or even a sensational twist for the story. The results of such publishing can cast a judgment upon a school or district which will remain for years. Thus, one school may be glorified while another may appear to be losing its accreditation.

The evaluators of school programs must consider carefully how to communicate with each group, teachers, board members, administrators, parents, and community. Each group has different interests and responsibilities for the school, and a different view about what is useful and meaningful to know about the school program.

ISSUE 12: VALID OBJECTIVES

Matching outcomes to objectives is a simple and direct view of evaluation (Tyler, 1949). However, there are problems with such obvious things as objectives. Some programs may not have written objectives. Many sets of written objectives are collections of program slogans and jargon which imply special meanings for otherwise commonly used words. Or, the written objectives are formal statements about what practitioners believe they should say, often selected from commercial or published authorities and usually agreed upon in a kind of negotiated consensus among program participants. Such statements are several levels more abstract and out of translation with what the instructors actually believe and do.

An evaluator like Scriven (1972) suggests goal-free evaluation to avoid objectives altogether. He uses the analogy of the double-blind testing of drugs by the Food and Drug Administration as a means to measure effects without being biased by prior knowledge of the purpose. Practically, however, the objectives matching outcomes is too generally accepted and too charming in its scientific engineering analogy to avoid. It makes practical sense.

If you evaluate using this congruence model, it may be helpful to work with the items of teacher made tests used in the curriculum. These items are more likely to express the valid intentions and imply the objectives for learning which the instructors hold. A second very productive approach is to collect test items from a commercial source. If the instructors can sort such items and identify twenty or thirty of the ones which best represent the program they teach, these may be a credible means to assess the objectives of the program.

ISSUE 13: A COPY IS ON FILE

Much educational evaluation is a perfunctory, time-consuming effort which interferes with the energy and attention of instructors, and is finally over when the report is typed, sent, and filed.

Too often this is a practical view of evaluation. Some of the reasons may be that a central or governmental bureaucracy required the evaluation, or no one had any commitment to the evaluation question posed, or the decision had already been made, or program people were not ready to evaluate.

Evaluation is such a costly use of time, energy, and interference with teaching and learning that program people must find it meaningful. We should take the time for the dialogue about important questions to develop before we use our energies in evaluation.

ISSUE 14: THE TYRANNY OF RISING EXPECTATIONS

An anthropologist might say that education is America's "magic." Whatever social ill we are revisiting in our country's historical cycle, from human rights, racial relations, the environment, poverty, global education, getting a job, competence, to wisdom of the ages, perhaps if we shake a little education at it, that will make it right.

As successful as education has been in the United States, the margins for advancement become narrow. Like the winning sports tradition of a great university, there is a tyranny of expectations. For example, a school reports that 96 percent of the student membership has not served detention this year. If that is a goal, there is not much room to work for improvement.

Improving on excellent does not allow much margin, but perhaps we could communicate and present what we do for better understanding. Being all things to all vested publics is to live in a tyranny. Schools must set their mission and their educational goals as meaningful and realistic, and then use evaluation as feedback to achieve them.

RECOGNIZING ISSUES

Issues do not arise in the practice of curriculum evaluation in a predictable order, nor can they be organized into a single conceptual framework. A useful way to think about issues is the following set of questions: (1) What is the purpose for evaluating? (2) What is the political/environmental context? (3) Are the evaluation procedures appropriate? (4) What meaning can be gained from the evaluation? With these questions in mind, issues can be recognized, clarified, and steps taken to minimize the harmful impact on an evaluation process.

SUMMARY

In planning and conducting an evaluation, issues are apt to arise which often draw our attention to the purposes for which we are evaluating, the political context within which we are working, the appropriateness of our procedures and ways of working, and the kinds of meaning which can be derived from an evaluation.

This chapter describes fourteen critical issues in evaluation:

1. Evaluating too soon may be a problem.
2. Evaluating a non-event is something talked about, perhaps, but never implemented.
3. Comparisons are never fair because one curriculum is not equal to another.
4. No change can be measured, but teachers perceive subtle differences.
5. A skeptical attitude of authorities regarding a program affects all evidence.
6. Evaluating as a strategy to get a certain outcome is mere deception.
7. We often miss the most valuable interpretations of an evaluation.
8. Evaluators from inside and outside a program offer important balance.
9. Evaluation is often started to find something wrong, resulting in well founded defensiveness by the staff.
10. Data can be used to create many different meanings, some of them wrong.
11. Putting evaluation interpretations in the media for all practical purposes makes them true.
12. Objectives are often not the true structure of a program.
13. Evaluation is often a legal or bureaucratic job to get finished instead of a search for improvement.

14. Rising expectations make even good programs subject to regular criticism by community members and clients.

Suggested Study Activities

1. Read a curriculum evaluation report and list one or two issues that might have been impacting on the study. Identify what evidence in the report is the basis for your opinion.
2. Read a curriculum evaluation report and discuss how the process would have been changed if an issue had been impacting on the procedure.
3. Interview an educator engaged in an evaluation study to find out what practical issues are being identified and how they are being resolved.
4. Survey board members, administrators, and teachers to identify which of the 14 issues in this chapter are of priority or significance. Compare the viewpoints of the three roles.
5. Review articles and texts to generate a list of issues related to curriculum evaluation.
6. Describe the one or two issues which are most relevant to an evaluation study you are presently conducting, and tell about the effort you are making in response to them.

Self-Assessment

1. Can you describe each of the curriculum evaluation issues in this chapter?
2. Can you explain a practical response to each issue which will minimize its harmful impact on an evaluation process?
3. Which of the issues in this chapter are most related to the question of:
   a. Evaluation purpose?
   b. Political/environmental context?
   c. Evaluation procedure?
   d. The meaning of the evaluation?

Bibliography

Charters, W. W., Jr. and Jones, J. E. On the Risk of Appraising Non-events in Program Evaluation. *Educational Researcher,* 1973, Vol. 2, No. 11, 5–7.

Hall, Gene E. and Louks, S. F. A Developmental Model for Determining Whether the Treatment is Actually Implemented. *American Educational Research Journal,* 1977, Vol. 14, No. 3, 263–276.

Kinghorn, John R. We Agree Workshop for Small-Group Leaders Plus Two Additional Group Skill Activities. /I/D/E/A Staff Paper, Dayton, Ohio: Institute for Development of Educational Activities, Inc., August, 1974.

Sava, Samuel G. Forward to Basics. *Vital Speeches,* 1975, Vol. 49, No. 7, 219–222.

Scriven, M. Pros and Cons About Goal-free Evaluation. *Evaluation Comment* Vol. 3, No. 1, 1–4, 1972.

Stufflebeam, Daniel I., et al. *Educational Evaluation and Decision Making.* Itasca, Ill.: F. E. Peacock Publishers, 1971.

Tyler, Ralph W. *Basic Principles of Curriculum and Instruction.* Chicago: University of Chicago Press, p. 105.

Chapter 5

CHOOSING THE
CURRICULUM EVALUATION MODEL

As a result of this chapter, the reader should be able to:

1. Describe the relevance of a model to evaluation planning.
2. Identify each evaluation model by its name, underlying assumptions, and purpose.
3. Explain the advantages and disadvantages of each evaluation model.
4. Give examples of situations most appropriate for the use of each evaluation model.

"The purposes of a model are to help us organize what we already know, to help us see new relationships, and to keep us from being dazzled by the full-blown complexity of the subject. A model is not intended to be a picture of reality but a tool for thinking."

Herbert Puryear

The word "model" appears by usage to mean a miniaturized version as in a model airplane, an idealized example such as a fashion model, or a form or pattern upon which real items can be developed. As models for curriculum evaluation are discussed in this chapter, we will be using the definition of a form or pattern upon which real evaluation plans can be shaped.

The "models" or approaches presented are not mutually exclusive options. Also, model means here a difference in approach and not a complete pattern to follow. Each model addresses different functions of curriculum evaluation and is based upon different assumptions. As you develop your own curriculum evaluation plan and procedure, you may find the models useful as guides for organizing and thinking about your evaluation effort.

Each model or approach will be described according to its purpose, its key components and assumptions, its advantages, and its disadvantage.

OBJECTIVES/OUTCOMES MODEL

This model is mainly a measurement of learner achievements related to the stated purposes and objectives of the curriculum. The attention to objectives in education by such authorities as Tyler (1949), Bloom (1956), Mager (1962), and Popham (1970), is well known. More recently English (1982) has incorporated this model into a system referred to as "curriculum management."

The key components of the objectives/outcomes curriculum evaluation model are the stated goals and educational objectives of the program, the instructional objectives which further specify the educational objectives, and the testing and measuring of student achievements.

The assumptions of the model are that the educational program is a rather close fitting procedure of getting student learning to be congruent with education objectives. It also assumes that the ends of learner outcomes of a program are the best measure of a program's effectiveness. It also assumes that the stated goals are the significant program objectives. A less explicit assumption which is easy to slip into is the notion of cause and effect. The curriculum program between the goals and the student achievement is the cause of that achievement. This has made the objectives/outcomes evaluation model particularly appealing for accountability movements.

Such evaluation processes are usually conducted by school district administrators, and in some cases as in competency-based education by state departments of education. Many federal and state supported projects require an objectives/outcomes form of evaluation. Evaluations are usually reported to school staffs, to the board of education, and to the community often through mass media forms.

The strengths of an evaluation plan based on the objectives/outcomes model are:

1. It is the most popular and widely used form of educational evaluation.
2. The outcomes are usually quantifiable as scores and measures enhancing the notions of objectivity.
3. It can direct the attention of the staff to the demonstration of the learning outcomes.

Limitations of an evaluation plan based on an objectives/outcomes model are:

1. The questions of why the curriculum is effective or what parts of it are influential can never be known. The curriculum and instruction are

seen as the "black box" treatment, which "causes" the attainment of outcomes.

2. Many schools using an outcomes assessment evaluation choose a well known standardized test, and assume that it is related to goals and objectives of the learning program. The model of curriculum evaluation for such schools is an *outcomes model* only, *not* an objectives/ outcomes model.

3. The information gained from the evaluation is rarely used for curriculum improvement. The information really does not address questions about *how* the curriculum program functions.

4. In the case of administering a well known standardized test as the outcomes measure, the true goals of the program may become those implied by the standardized test itself.

DECISION-MAKING MODEL

Stufflebeam (1971) has defined evaluation as the "science of providing information for decision making." His explanation of evaluation is probably the most conceptually based, and comes closest to being appropriately called a model. Its framework tends to explain and classify other models in curriculum evaluation. This comprehensive view and persuasive base makes the Decision-Making Model one of the most appealing for administrators and program managers.

The basis of Stufflebeam's work is found in a two by two table as in Table 4.

It was Ralph Tyler (1949, p. 63) who said that the ends of education make up the domain of curriculum. The means of education make up the domain of instruction. That is an easy and useful division for thinking about Table 4. Stufflebeam noted that the educational program has an intended form and an actual reality. Every teacher who has planned a lesson and proceeded to put it into action in the classroom is well aware of the distinction between intended and actual.

Stufflebeam identifies the area of program of ends intended as the search for valid purposes. He identifies the decision of this quadrant as the purposing decision, and the question to be addressed as, "What shall we do?" The providing of information to make the purposing decision he calls Context Evaluation. The intended means area of the quadrant deals with structuring decisions, the "How will we do it?" question.

Table 4
Basis of the Decision Making Model

	Intended	Actual
Curriculum Ends	Context Evaluation	Product Evaluation
Curriculum Means	Input Evaluation	Process Evaluation

Providing information for this type of decision is referred to as Input Evaluation.

Actual Means by which the program functions relate to implementing decisions, the "Are we doing it?" question. The providing of information for implementing decisions is referred to as Process Evaluation. The actual ends of the program relate to recycling decisions, the "Have we done it?" question. Providing information for these kinds of decisions is called Product Evaluation. Thus, the acronym C.I.P.P., Context, Input, Process, and Product, is often used to describe the decision-making model proposed by Stufflebeam.

Other authors, notably Provus (1971), developed strategies in the category called Decision-Making Model of Evaluation. Provus focuses with more emphasis on the discrepancies or gaps which may occur between intended and actual states of the program and the ends and means. He also identifies the three decision options as: (1) maintain the program; (2) change the program; or (3) terminate the program. Stufflebeam's more conceptual basis for the change options in decision making were: (1) maintain (no change); (2) improve the program (incremental change), or (3) major revision (large change); and (4) a complete renewal, or metamorphosis which he suggested was only theoretical.

It is easy to see the objectives/outcomes model of evaluation as a subset of the C.I.P.P. model involving Context Evaluation to establish the objectives and Product Evaluation as the outcomes measurement.

The Decision-Making Model is based upon the assumption that decision making can be conducted in logical, rational, and sequential manner. It also assumes that the evaluation process can be included and resourced as a continuous component of the operations system of a program.

This decision model of evaluation is most often adopted as a practice or at least a viewpoint by administrators and program managers. The attention to each phase of the program development and the notions of decision points is particularly appealing to those responsible for program leadership.

Advantages of the decision-making model of curriculum evaluation are that it provides a framework of explanation for different kinds of information gathering for each phase of the program. It may help educators to view decision making in a more rational, logical way. It explains the apparent relationship between needs assessment, quality control, and testing programs to measure outcomes.

The limitations of the decision-making model for evaluation are that decision making is often political, often not a clear and uncluttered point in a flow chart of events. Regarding issues of curriculum evaluation, the decision making model can be used as a rationalization of solutions already chosen by intuition, personal bias, or political expediency. Another limitation is that often the information which can be gathered in time to aid the decision making is insufficient. A further difficulty is that the evaluation process can provide information, but it can never relieve the decision maker of the personal sorting, the judging, the realizing, the choosing, and the responsibility for the decision. Finally, there is often little budget or institutional support for a continuous attention to evaluation.

RESPONSIVE EVALUATION MODEL

Responsive evaluation is that system of providing information in response to requests and requirements by the program personnel, the users. It always focuses upon activities and happenings rather than what was planned or intended. It also accounts for the value differences, issues, and conflicts within the program as it is occurring. The main purposes served by responsive evaluation are for problem solving, stimulating communication among the program related persons, and assessing the development and implementation level of the program or curriculum.

Robert Stake is one of the major authors proposing this kind of evaluation. His approach is to identify the logical relationship between the antecedents, transactions and outputs of the intended program and the observed program, and to facilitate a discussion of meaning of this information and its congruence among the program personnel.

A varied form of responsive evaluation has been identified as Transactional Evaluation. Rippey differentiates Transactional Evaluation from other forms of formative evaluation in that it includes viewpoints of the curriculum program initiators as well as program implementors, and attends to the nature of change as it influences the organization and the curriculum being implemented. Its particular benefit is to clarify issues and attitudes for and against the curriculum implementation rather than to ignore or attempt to coerce reluctant users or unconscious saboteurs of a curriculum implementation. It can be very helpful in determining what the values and commitment are, and what intervening variables and unintended consequences are influencing the implementation.

Responsive evaluation is often provided by an external evaluator or consultant to the program. It may also be included as an informal part of the leadership role of a curriculum program. This, however, is a little like wearing two hats; one as initiator and the other as a listener/counselor to the staff.

The assumptions of responsive evaluation are that an openness and flexibility about the implementation of a curriculum exists among leadership and staff. Another premise is that airing the inconsistencies and biases can lead to growth and development of the organization. A third premise is that program personnel can make requests for evaluative information about significant issues.

The strengths of this approach are that it is very consistent with principles inherent in the concept of feedback. It offers a way to deal with issues of curriculum implementation.

JUDGMENT MODEL

The nature of judgment can be best explained when considered with opinion and with fact. If we consider Figure 2, an opinion may be held in a very superficial way on a minimum of evidence, and on the basis of attitude preference and bias. A fact on the other extreme is also particular, but may be based on some quantified or identified evidence; it tends to be more objectifiable. A judgment is a reasoned and logically developed conclusion which is/has dealt with multiple opinions and facts. So, for example, "Jimmy is a smart boy" may be an opinion based on a casual meeting or observation. "Jimmy got a score in the ninth stanine on a math test" is a fact. "Jimmy got an A grade for this term in math" is the result of a judgment made by a professional teacher based upon activities, responses, homework, tests, and performances. It is a considered and reasonable conclusion reached.

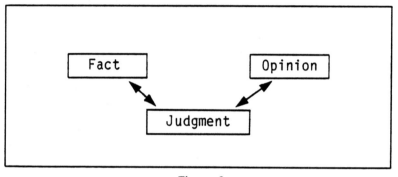

Figure 2
The Nature of Judgment

The judgment model is an appraisal and recommendation procedure performed by persons selected for that responsibility. Sometimes persons are selected on the basis of whom they represent, for example, the community citizens task group of the board of education. Sometimes persons are selected for their prominence and status rather than whom they would seem to represent. Other persons may be selected for a judgment evaluation because of their expertise.

Three specific examples of the judgment model of curriculum evaluation are: (1) the blue ribbon panel; (2) the accreditation evaluation procedure; and (3) the connoisseurship evaluation strategy suggested by Elliott Eisner (1979). The blue ribbon panel may be appointed, for example, by the governor to investigate and make recommendation on discipline in school for the purpose of establishing policy. The accreditation evaluation procedure involves the establishment of standards and criteria for institutional members of an accrediting agency. At regular intervals, say five or ten years, a self-study is conducted by staff of a member institution based upon the accrediting standards. This is culminated by a report and an accrediting team visitation to the institution. The third example of connoisseurship is a form of judgmental criticism offered by someone so expert in the field that he or she would be considered a critic in the same sense that one would view an arts critic of a fine arts show.

Who would likely use the judgment model? The blue ribbon panel can be thought of as potential for the school board or superintendent. Schools, colleges, and other educational agencies are familiar with the accreditation process. The connoisseurship strategy might be employed in a peer-supervision process between teachers who have demonstrated high levels of the craft and art of teaching.

The assumptions of the judgment model are that professional experience and citizens by personally representing a segment of the community can make reasoned and value-based judgments which will identify direction and improvement possibilities of curriculum programs.

The strength of the judgment model is its involvement of respected persons and its internal and external validating procedure in the accreditation example.

Its limitations are that an individual person never quite represents a constituency. A second limitation is that persons of status or expertise when confronted with a new situation or knowledge area may be very unprepared. For instance, the blue ribbon panel who reports recommendations on discipline in the classroom may seem naive and absurd to the classroom teachers.

The Connoissuership Model is described as the criticism which can be provided by the subjective impressions and judgments of an outstanding expert or true artist in the field. The analogy is used of the behavior and skill of a literary critic to explain this approach. The strength of this approach lies in the repertoire and subtlety of the expert. Its weakness may be in the subjectivity of impressions.

The Adversarial Evaluation Model is implemented by means of two separate evaluations conducted with equal resources by those who advocate the program and those who do not. A "jury" is appointed to hear the reports and make a decision in favor of or against the program. In a true sense the Adversary Model belongs in the Judgment Model category. The problems of the Adversary Model are obvious in the political nature of decision making about educational programs and policy. It also expends finances for two competing efforts to evaluate which may appear to be uneconomical.

RESEARCH MODEL

The Goal-free Evaluation Model by Scriven is developed to avoid the biases of the intentions or stated objectives of a curriculum. Scriven uses the analogy of the testing of drugs for their effects by double-blind experimental procedures offers the consumer a safer and more credible basis for using medications. Likewise, he suggests that curriculum effects should be investigated without the bias of claims and intentions. This approach truly falls under the category of a Research Model for curriculum evaluation. Such a model describes rigorous and controlled procedures to discover how programs work and with what effect. The Research Model is best applied to efforts to improve or conceptualize new designs and new methods of instruction.

MAKING A CHOICE

A model is selected as a guide to curriculum evaluation planning for these reasons; that situational cues of issues suggest it as the best approach, the assumptions of the model fit the expressed need for the evaluation, the advantages of using the approach are persuasive, or the client wants the evaluator to use a certain approach. Table 5 can be very helpful in making a decision about which Model approach to follow in developing and implementing an evaluation study. While surveying the situation and talking with clients, the evaluator can examine situational cues, assumptions the clients have about evaluation, and the advantages and disadvantages of each approach. Once a broad choice is made about the model to follow, the examples listed and the major authors of the table can be used to search the literature for designs and records of actual cases. This review can then prepare one to plan and implement procedures for evaluation as described in Part II which follows.

SUMMARY

The purposes of a model are to help us organize what we know, and to help us plan and carry out an evaluation without getting distracted by the complexity of the situation. Thinking about each model can help clarify the purposes and assumptions for doing an evaluation. Choosing a model or approach to follow in planning an evaluation is a decision

Table 5
Choosing an Appropriate Evaluation Model

MODEL	EXAMPLES	AUTHORS	ASSUMPTIONS	CHOICE ADVANTAGES	CHOICE DISADVANTAGES	SITUATIONAL CUES FOR CHOOSING THE MODEL
Objectives/ Outcomes	Competency Based Education Technical Subjects Curricula Skills based programs	Tyler Bloom Popham Provus Mager	- congruence - means are separate from and causative of ends - learner outcomes are the best measure of a curriculum - the stated goals are the true program goals - particular outcomes are significant	- Widely used - quantitive outcomes are accepted as objective - staff attention is directed to outcomes	- narrow focus - no explanation of program dynamics	- low expectations for Learners - a call for basics curriculum - great differences between formal and instructional curriculum - a call for accountability
Decision Making	Systems approach to curriculum development	Stufflebeam Alkin	- decision making is rational and logical	- enhances the view of program management and improvement - promotes the view of efficient and effective school leadership	- decision making is often political - Information cannot be gathered in time - continuous stages of evaluation may not have support	- curriculum development will require long term as well as yearly plans
Responsive Evaluation	Transactional Evaluation Organization Development in Schools Problem Solving in Curriculum and Staff Development	Stake Rippey	- that open communication can be helpful to personnel conflict - airing biases can lead to growth and development	- very consistent with a human relations approach - works toward staff problem solving skills	- needs outside consultant - people tend to avoid the basic issues	- innovative curriculum implementation is underway - faculty burnout is obvious - conflict and tension are apparent in working relationships - communications are closed off
Judgment	Blue Ribbon Panel Accreditation Boards Review School Self-Study Adversarial Evaluation Connoisseurship	Owens Eisner	- consensus of status group is valid - expertise can solve problems	- expertise can be used - recommendations can be made in timely fashion - political base for decision making	- experts and status persons may be inept on unfamiliar topics and subject fields	- curriculum changes which will affect the community when (political) choices must be made (e.g., school closing, sex education, drug abuse)
Research	Goal Free Evaluation Instructional Research Learner Validation of New Curricula	Scriven Campbell Stanley	- critical variables can be examined	- some rigor to the study - minimizes bias	- halo effect of a test can achieve more than the critical variable	- research and development of New Curricular Designs

reached by considering the purpose for the evaluation and the assumptions or expectations of people involved.

The models of value for evaluation which have been discussed are: the objectives/outcomes model and the decision making model, the responsive evaluation model, the judgment model, and the research model.

Suggested Activities

1. Interview a principal or a department head about strengths and concerns they have about a curriculum. Decide which model would be most appropriate upon which to pattern an evaluation study based upon his/her comments.
2. Make a matrix of the evaluation models and contrast the functions, purpose, assumptions of each.
3. Examine published evaluation reports to determine which model was used as a background.
4. Examine federal and state regulations for funded projects to note what assumptions and model are being expressed or implied for evaluation.
5. Read all the scholarly literature you can find on one model and write a paper on your findings.

Self Assessment

1. Can you explain why and how a model is useful in evaluation planning?
2. Can you explain the purpose and assumptions of each model described?
3. Can you explain the advantages and disadvantages of each model?
4. Can you suggest examples of what occasions and evaluation needs would be best suited for each evaluation model?

References

Bloom, Benjamin S. Taxonomy of Educational Objectives: The Classification of Educational Goals. Handbook I. Cognitive Domain. New York: David McKay, 1956.

Eisner, Elliot W. The Educational Imagination: On the Design and Evaluation of Educational Programs. New York: McMillan Company, 1979.

English, Fenwick W. and Steffy, Betty E. Curriculum as a Strategic Management Tool, *Educational Leadership*, Vol. 39, No. 4, January 1982, pp. 276–278.

Mager, Robert F. Preparing Instructional Objectives. Palo Alto, California: Fearon Publishers, 1962.

Popham, W. James and Baker, Eva L. Establishing Instructional Goals. Englewood Cliffs, New Jersey: Prentice-Hall, Inc., 1970.

Provus, M. Discrepancy Evaluation: For Educational Program Improvement and Assessment. Berkeley, California: McCutchan, 1971.

Stufflebeam, Daniel I. et al. Educational Evaluation and Decision Making. Itasca, Illinois: F. E. Peacock Publishers, Inc., 1971.

Tyler, Ralph W. Basic Principles of Curriculum and Instruction. Chicago: The University of Chicago Press, 1949.

Worthen, B. R. and Rogers, W. T. The Pitfalls and Potential of Adversary Evaluation, *Educational Leadership*, Vol. 37, April 1980, pp. 536–543.

Rippey, R. M. (Ed.) Studies in Transactional Evaluation, Berkeley, Calif.: McCutchan, 1973.

Stake, R. E. The Countenance of Educational Evaluation. Teachers College Record, Vol. 68, 1967.

Scriven, M. Prose and Cons about Goal-Free Evaluation. *Evaluation Comment.* Vol., 3, No. 4, 1972.

Part II

PROCEDURES FOR CURRICULUM EVALUATION

Chapter 6

IS THE CURRICULUM REALLY IMPLEMENTED?

As a result of studying this chapter, the reader should be able to:

1. Define and give examples of *levels of reality* in program implementation.
2. Describe some of the developments in the effort to measure the implementation of educational programs.
3. Identify and explain each of the steps to be taken in developing a plan for the assessment of the implementation of a curriculum program.
4. Explain some implications of levels of curriculum implementation and the appropriateness of evaluation of this same curriculum.

There exists a school in session which is clean and well cared for in its building and grounds, where talented teachers, capable and spirited youngsters, and concerned and supportive parents carry out their various roles and responsibilities for good teaching and learning. In the front yard of this school is a very large wooden sign on two posts and two bolted crossboards made, no doubt, in the school's woodworking shop. The two crossboards have letters routed in them to spell out COMMUNITY on the top board and MIDDLE SCHOOL on the bottom board. These routed letters are painted white and the whole effect is an attractive presentation.

If you walk around behind this sign and look at the bottom board, you can see through a coat of brown paint the routed letters which spell out JR HIGH SCHOOL. Some time in the past this was the junior high school. When a decision was made to have a middle school instead of a junior high, the bottom board was turned over and routed in the school shop and bolted back on its posts. Now just suppose that the sign was the only thing about the school which was ever changed!

The middle school concept is developed around learners of a certain age range, a personalized learning experience process involving choice and planning of goals and learning objectives, collaboration or teaming between teachers for integrated subject areas, and flexible scheduling for a more fitting curricular experience for learners. Should we assume that all these components of a middle school program exist and are functioning because the sign in front of the school has been changed? Should we accept a charge by the board of education to evaluate the effects of the middle school program on learners and assume from the school sign that the program is at work as the independent variable which is influencing the experiences, attitudes, and learning behaviors of these young people? We obviously would need a great deal of information about whether the program is implemented and how it works to evaluate the effects of a middle school program.

Likewise, a curriculum cannot be assumed to be implemented because the teachers refer to it by a particular name and have boxes and shelves of purchased materials by the same name. There are many conditions which must be present for a curriculum to be implemented. Some of these are: an understanding of the design of the curriculum, a valuing of the curriculum by staff; financial, personnel, and policy commitment by the school board; organizational support and leadership by the school principal; inservice support and skills and understanding of supervisors; and perhaps most critical to outcomes, new or changed teaching behaviors by instructors, and new or changed classroom behaviors by learners. In this chapter we will develop an organized way to examine whether the curriculum is implemented, which is the context to be established before curriculum evaluation activities are undertaken.

NONEVENTS IN
CURRICULUM DEVELOPMENT AND EVALUATION

The study of implementation conditions of a curriculum perhaps began with the realization that curricula may have changed in name only, and that the differences in the actual teaching and learning in the classroom may have changed not at all. This may explain some of the results of no significant difference in learner outcomes when programs are compared or evaluated.

The original attention to this area of nonevents (nothing really happened) can be attributed to W. W. Charters, Jr. and John Jones at the Center for Educational Policy and Management in Oregon. In their effort to evaluate the innovation of differentiated staffing, they became aware that no actual changes in behavior of individuals had occurred between experimental and control schools even though persons in the experimental school could talk about the concept of differential staffing and some organizational arrangements and titles of jobs had been changed to reflect the design.

It was through a follow-up study of this innovation that different *levels of reality* of a program were identified. These levels of program description were called: (1) Institutional Commitment; (2) Structural Context; (3) Role Performance (staff perspective); and (4) Learning Activities (student perspective). Institutional Commitment was described as the formal and authoritative decision and commitment to pursue a program. Structural Context was explained as the organizational, staffing, and resource configuration of the program. Role Performance was defined as the behavioral changes and functions of teachers as they actively plan and teach. Learner Activities was defined as the behavior changes, activities and experiences of learners. Charters and Jones also noted that the program implementation not only seemed to have at least these four levels of description, but that the implementation is also subject to forces beyond the program itself which they referred to as extraneous determinants. They also pointed out that the implementation of the program at these various levels may generate consequences unintended by the program design which will impact on further levels of the program implementation. For instance, a program which structurally arranges for time and organization for teachers to consult with each other and make planning decisions, can affect the decision making role and leadership approach of the school principal (perhaps an unintended consequence of implementation). Such a change might invoke principal behaviors which in the long run could be self-limiting to the curriculum program itself. The figure below illustrates the ideas of this complex view of program implementation (Charter and Jones, 1973).

This analysis of implementation makes rather clear that student outcomes are the consequence of a very complex and interrelated set of conditions. An evaluation of student outcomes without first considering whether any conditions of a new curriculum exist in the school program provides no evidence of quality of the learning experience or accountability in the curriculum.

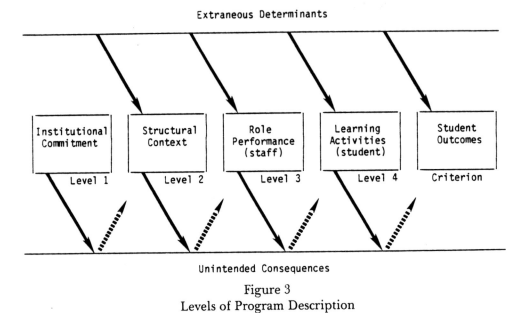

Figure 3
Levels of Program Description

REFINEMENT OF THE LEVELS OF REALITY

A year long case study of these levels of program description in program implementation (Kohler, 1976) provides further insight into the dynamics of implementation as well as a definition of the levels.

Level 1—Commitment

Commitment seems to have two forms. The commitments of the institution to pursue a curriculum or program are the formal policy statements, endorsements and recommendations, and the commitment of funds for staffing and other resources. The second component of commitment is staff commitment to pursue the program. That is, the teachers and principal value this program, find it compatible with their own philosophy of teaching, believe it will work, and are committed to pursue it and implement it. Of all the components of program description, this appears to be the most critical. Simply said, if teachers believe in it and are committed, they can overcome many obstacles, they will turn situations into resources, and they will convince others of the program's value. If, on the other hand, they are skeptical or divided in their commitment, no amount of resources or incentives, leadership or coercion, will result in a complete implementation and meaningful program. Many a program, we suppose, has existed in state and federal reports, in inservice materials and classroom texts which never existed in the hearts of teachers. Evidences of implementation of such programs are likely to be mostly sham. On the other hand, committed teachers have carried programs long after resources were withdrawn, and even where administrators were appointed and directed to eliminate a curriculum or program.

Level 2—Organizational Context

This level has been renamed for clarity. It includes those policy, personnel, organizational, inservice, staff development, and material resources which can be acquired or arranged administratively. This program level can often be accomplished by an administrator without much concern about what behaviors the teachers have acquired or to which they are committed. Thus, a middle school's organizational chart may show teachers arranged by teams. This by no means should imply that teachers can or will work together in team roles and functions. It is, as a matter of fact, quite common for teamed teachers who are uncomfortable with the organization to carry out a collaborative curriculum program *for show* and a second self-contained classroom curriculum by which they actually teach to their own subjects or textbooks. Such dual programs are very wearying not only for their double work investment, but for the tensions produced in representing something which is not authentic and which does not have their commitment.

Level 3—Teacher Roles and Responsibilities

This level is concerned, by and large, with what Goodlad called the instructional curriculum. At this level we want to assess whether teachers have the skills to carry out the new curriculum and whether they, in fact, perform with new or changed behaviors. In the team teaching example used previously, we would be assessing whether teachers are trained effectively to perform in team situations, and whether they do, in fact, use these skills in planning, interacting, and evaluating instruction.

When observable teacher behaviors have changed, we can begin to look for changes in the learning experience for students. If teacher behaviors are exactly the same as with a past curriculum, there is very little reason to believe that learner outcomes such as achievement, attitudes, and productivity will change.

Level 4—Learner Roles and Responsibilities

We too often assume that learners are dependent variables in the learning equation. That is, if we teachers initiate something in the classroom, the learner will react in an appropriate way, and learning will take place. We have little hope that learning outcomes will change in terms of knowledge, skills, or attitudes, unless attitudes and behaviors of learners in the classroom are observed to change. Teachers have only indirect influence in this process by arranging activities and structure. It is the learner who copes, strategizes, remembers, inquires, makes application, and arrives at new meaning and perspective. When the learner can be observed or can relate new behaviors of learning, new awareness of learning how to learn with the changed curriculum, we can look for changes in outcomes. Until this experiential curriculum of the learner is in place, there will likely be no significant difference in learning between the new and the old curriculum.

If we take this level of implementation seriously, it is quite a practical idea to plan for "inservice" activities for learners as well as teachers. The learners do indeed need to become aware and to practice the new skills of learning which a change in the curriculum implies.

ATTEMPTS TO MEASURE CURRICULUM IMPLEMENTATION

Several developments to measure curriculum implementation followed the work of Charters and Jones. Three of these are worth mention here for their particular methods in addressing the problem.

Leonard and Lowery compared a BSCS Green Version (biology) laboratory program with an Extended Discretion Model laboratory program through an experimental treatment design. To verify that the two programs were indeed different treatments in practice, they reviewed the conceptual description of each program (the Ideal Curriculum) and identified differences which they perceived would follow consistently from these two programs in the observable teacher-student behaviors. This list of observable behaviors differing for each program was then given definition, cues, and ground rules for an interaction analysis observation system patterned after the Flanders approach to time interval assessment in the classroom. An observation schedule of the teacher-student behaviors in each laboratory setting was carried out by two observers to assure reliability. The interpretation of the observations was that the two independent variables (the curriculum treatments) were significantly different in observable teacher-student behaviors. As has been noted before, until teacher behaviors and student behaviors change at the instructional and experiential curriculum levels, there is little prospect that there will be any consequent change in learner outcomes. Indeed this contention is supported again by the significant difference which was found in student outcomes between the two treatments in this study.

This investigation took a very limited view of the independent variables which may be found in different curricula. There is in this study very little effort to persuade as to why these teacher-student behaviors were crucial to the outcomes of the treatments. Nevertheless, we can take from this study the following notions: (1) That the "Ideal Curriculum" level of a program, the conceptual design, can be analyzed for its implications of pertinent behaviors at the instructional and experiential levels. The ideal design can suggest what types of concrete behaviors would be consistent at other curriculum levels. (2) That observation methods already at hand can be adapted for specific uses in evaluating curriculum implementation. (3) That observation by two people is one of the easier ways to address a basic issue of evaluation like reliability.

Hall and Loucks (1974) have contributed the concept and methodology for Levels of Use to this issue of implementation. Levels of Use (LOU) establishes a method for documenting reliably eight different levels of use of an innovation with several categories of personal behavior. The system is predominantly a cognitive view of change and adoption of an innovation, and focuses only on the teacher and the decision points that this person passes through in undertaking a new curriculum. The method used in assessment is an open type of interview lasting about twenty minutes which is tape recorded and permits the teacher to describe his or her activity and use of an innovation. A review of this tape by two trained classifiers can result in a reliable classification of where the teacher's use of the innovation is regarding the eight levels and the various categories of specific teacher behavior.

The advantage of this system is that it is generic to many or all classroom innovations, and it can be used without the investigator having much background in the particular innovation. The relation of the

Levels of Use classification to achievement outcomes consequent to an innovation is complex. This may be because the number of levels of use is large. Basically, the research on the (LOU) system has established a general relationship between achievement outcomes and levels of use.

The contribution of this system to the assessment of curriculum implementation is that first, the system is generic, it can be used with many innovations. It is free of any category definitions which must be changed or revised because of any specific innovation. Second, the system uses a time saving, open interview method to obtain data. This system also has undergone a validation study using classroom observation methods to verify the type of use found in the classroom.

One limitation of the (LOU) system for assessing implementation is that it focuses only on the instructional curriculum level. We know nothing about the organizational level, the level of commitment by either teachers or administrators, and we know nothing from it about the way learners behave regarding the innovations. Thus, the hidden structural assumptions which may be implied from such a system are: (1) that the teacher is the accountable person for the innovation, and (2) that the learner is basically a reactor or dependent variable to be influenced and to respond appropriately to the teacher's behaviors. And if the teacher behavior is so central to the implementation, as certainly it is, then Kohler's study would suggest we must know a great deal about the teacher's valuing and commitment which are beyond the categories of the Levels of Use instrument. A further limitation of the (LOU) system is that in studying a general systems or "bundle of variables" innovation such as IGE (Individually Guided Education) the researchers were unable to examine the whole innovation but separated out an instructional subpart of the system for examination. This reductionist view of parts of an innovation must surely alter the true picture about what is happening in curriculum implementation.

A third effort to assess program implementation is the "Survey of Effective School Processes" developed by the I/D/E/A affiliate of the Kettering Foundation. The survey system involves an interview plan with a central office administrator, the school principal, teachers, and students, as well as observation in classrooms and a parent questionnaire. The interview of the different roles within the school organization follows more nearly the levels of reality of program implementation suggested by Charters and Jones.

The interview process is guided by an open ended set of questions making the setting somewhat conversational as in the method by Hall and Loucks. The interview assessment guide contains suggestions of how to rate responses. The entire assessment of a school requires a minimum of two trained interviewers and a schedule of two or three days time (see the Case of the Weary Faculty in section three). The entire system involves temporary schedule changes in the school and considerable time of interviewers and some involvement of all staff. The payoff for such an investment is a complete involvement of staff in a dialogue about the school program and a preparation for goal setting or action planning for further program development.

The drawbacks to the Effective School Processes system are the need to have interviewers aware of the educational design involving 35 school program outcomes upon which the system is developed and the amount of time involved. The rating system takes some practice and the outcomes of the rating system for the interviews are more useful as interpretations and feedback to staff than they would be as specific scores for purposes of research on implementation.

A SYSTEMATIC LOOK AT CURRICULUM IMPLEMENTATION

A systematic plan to assess curriculum implementation must start with the assumption that curriculum change (in this case implementation) must be a change in people. And imply that people change is evidenced in three ways: knowledge, values, and behaviors. To some degree, people know about the curriculum design or they don't; they find the design of value and consistent with their own educational philosophy, and they are able to and do perform in changed ways based upon that new knowledge and values.

The second premise of a curriculum implementation assessment plan is related to the assumption about people and change. Knowledge and behaviors are things which people *can* do or perform, but values are things people *will* do. So people can comply with performances on call if they believe they are expected to or if an interviewer or observer leads or implies what responses are expected. The only authentic or "fidelity" responses of people involved in curriculum implementation are those that they choose and are committed to do. Therefore, an interview or observation method used to assess curriculum implementation must be open in structure and provide a means for the investigator to recognize the illustrations and cues which the implementors provide.

A third assumption of this approach to assessment of curriculum implementation is that actors in the different roles in the school setting each have influence in whether the curriculum gets implemented. So for instance, the central office supervisor should have knowledge of the curriculum design, should personally value the approach or philosophy of it, and should be able to affect the institutional aspects of commitment, resources, and organizational and staff support of the program. The principal should have knowledge of the curriculum design, find it personally consistent with his or her educational values, and be able to influence the organization, schedule, materials and resources, and the inservice and staff development, and the classroom and school environments which support the curriculum. The teacher should have knowledge of the curriculum design and value it as compatible with his/her own educational philosophy about teaching and learning, and be able to identify and to demonstrate the instructional behaviors which are necessary, the inservice needs, organizational resources, and curricular materials and classroom environments essential for this curriculum. At their level the students understand (knowledge) how the curriculum is used to learn, what relevance (personal value) it has for them, and what new behaviors and perspectives (how to learn this way) are needed for them to be successful. Lest this last role of learners sound too sophisticated, there are two reminders: first, this approach when adjusted to appropriate kinds of terms and language has been used with elementary children, and second, it is the bane of almost all teachers and adults generally that we set our expectations too low for what learners can understand and do.

This set of assumptions for assessing curriculum implementation accounts for all the significant direct and indirect roles of professionals and learners; it follows in a general way the levels of reality of program implementation suggested by Charters and Jones, it addresses the five components of the curriculum wheel, namely curriculum design, instructional method, resources, development, and learner experience; and it relies for evidence on the knowledge, values, and behaviors which people will voluntarily bring forth in interview or observation.

STEPS OF CURRICULUM
IMPLEMENTATION ASSESSMENT FOR PRACTICE

Up to this point the case has been developed that: (1) no curriculum evaluation project has much external validity until the quality of implementation of the curriculum is understood; (2) there are several good efforts to assess implementation available which can be adopted or adapted; and (3) the assumptions for an assessment of implementation would include the notions that change is a change in people; attitude is a primary factor; and all persons involved influence the implementation. From this point, a proposal follows by which an implementation assessment plan can be developed in steps.

Analysis of the Curriculum Design

The first step toward implementation assessment is to study and analyze the conception of the curriculum design (the Ideal Curriculum). The four phase curriculum matrix (see Chapter 2) is a useful tool for identifying the types of learning, learning strategies, teaching strategies, methods, and materials implied by the curriculum design. The curriculum wheel (see Chapter 2) may also be useful when thinking about the staff development and resources and materials which are necessary. When the curriculum design has been studied for its value and method, the investigators are ready to set expectations.

Assigning Expectations for Each Role and Level in Curriculum Implementation

The basic question guiding this step might be, "What should the person doing the job know, value, and be able to do regarding each of the levels of curriculum implementation?" For example, what should the central office supervisor, responsible for this curriculum program, know, value and be able to do regarding commitment, organizational level, instructional role and learner activities? Each role (principal, teacher and learner, and perhaps others) should be addressed similarly based upon the particular curriculum design. Parents, guidance counselors, and others, for instance, may have a role regarding a particular curriculum.

In the example of the central office supervisor, we might expect this person to understand the curriculum design, to find its philosophical basis personally compatible, and to know what institutional commitments of board and superintendent have been made and should be made in support of the program. The supervisor should know: (1) what aspects of the adopted district philosophy are in keeping with the curriculum design; (2) what formal step of adoption and support the board has taken regarding the curriculum; (3) the financial, staff, and resources needs; and (4) what the board of education and superintendent have done and need to do. If, for example, the curriculum design requires teaching aides, has the institutional commitment been made, or has this been shunted off to teachers or the PTA to find parent volunteers? The supervisor should also know the needs and developments of the school and classroom teachers for resources, inservice, and staff development. It would not be illustrative to carry the example of the supervisor much further because it is a very indirect role in affecting the conditions of the learning experience (experiential curriculum) in the classroom, but the example does illustrate the role responsibilities of each actor in the implementation process. The other roles of principal, teacher, and learner would have different expectations and increasingly direct influence on the learning experience. The supervisor may be assessed appropriately as having direct knowledge about institutional commitment and organizational level of the implementation and perceptions about the instructional level. The principal may be assessed appropriately as having direct knowledge of institutional commitment and organizational level of implementation, and perceptions about instructional level and learner's level. Teachers may be appropriately assessed as having perceptions about institutional commitment and organization, and direct knowledge of the teaching and learning levels. Learners may be assessed as having direct knowledge of the learning level and perceived knowledge of the teaching level of implementation.

Developing an Interview Protocol

A protocol should be developed for interviewing each of the major roles in the implementation of the curriculum. It should have an open question interview format permitting further probe questions, include examples of *look-for* evidence related to each question, and include a rating system on each of the implementation levels relevant to the role. Table 6 is a brief illustration of a protocol which might follow from the earlier example of the supervisor's role in curriculum implementation.

The rating scales for each implementation level or dimension within the interview are not so much a systematic way to quantify implementation as they are a way to consolidate with one expression a judgment about what was heard in the interview. The important outcome of the assessment of implementation is a good judgment (valid and reliable) about the state of the curriculum in use. The state of implementation of this curriculum then can indicate what types of evaluation projects are timely and useful.

Table 6

Curriculum Implementation Interview (Central Office Supervisor)

Begin with a suitable acquaintance or sharing exchange followed by:

Dimension	1) Suggested Questions(s) a) Follow-up or Probe Question(s)	("Listen For" Examples)
Personal Knowledge of the Curriculum Design	1) What is your understanding of this curriculum? a) How does it propose that learning best occurs? b) What types of teaching approaches are best for this curriculum?	- Learning theory described is consistent with concept of this curriculum. - Teaching approach is accurately understood - Supervisor response is thoughtful and not a rote response.
Personal Value of the Curriculum Design	1) How do you feel about this curriculum? a) How would it fit with your own teaching style? b) From your own philosophy of teaching, what would be of concern in this program?	- Positive about the curriculum. - Supervisor gives examples of having taught or would like to teach this way. - None or few issues with the basic values of the curriculum design.
Personal Behaviors of the Supervisor	1) What one or two things would you wish that you could do to improve this curriculum in the school?	- Listen for what goals or needs related to support of teaching and/or learning levels of implementation
Institutional Commitment Level of Implementation	1) When was this curriculum formally adopted the board of education? a) by memorandum, formal motion, - b) was a presentation made? 2) Did the board commit any funds for this implementation? a) For what? b) How much?	- Date, formal document, board minutes reference - Purchase of materials and books are common in support. Really meaningful commitment usually means staff personnel and funds for inservice and staff development.

Making a good judgment (valid and reliable) can be approached in the following ways: First, the overlapping interview about the levels of implementation with other role actors in the school (principal, teachers and others) provides a comparison from different perspectives. Consistency of such perceptions about implementation from different role perspectives is an acceptable kind of validity. Second, the question of reliability has been addressed by the previously cited studies in using pairs of interviewers or observers.

Interview or observation protocols would need to be developed for the principal, teachers, and learners at minimum. Interviewing of the principal need not take longer than the supervisor's interview, perhaps 20 minutes. All teachers involved with the curriculum should be interviewed, perhaps together, which may take longer because of the productive interaction which can be facilitated. Such a group setting may require an

Table 6 Continued

Dimension	1) Suggested Questions(s) a) Follow-up or Probe Question(s)	("Listen For" Examples)
Institutional Commitment Level of Implementation cont'd	3) What would you estimate the support of this kind of curriculum to be by the board, by the building leaders, all the teachers involved, the parents. (Interviewer marks an X on the Scale Regarding Institutional Commitment Level of Implementation) Little Partial Full Implementation Implementation Implementation 1-------2-------3-------4-------5-------6-------7	- Generally perceives support. - Community values are in keeping with this approach. - Principals understand it. - Teachers support it.

Organizational Level of	1) Were any school changes made for the curriculum to be used more effectively?
	
	2) Were materials or resources purchased for this curriculum?
	
	3) What sort of inservice and staff development are related to this curriculum?
	   a) Were there any visits from or to other schools?
	   b) Are there any follow-ups planned?
	
	(Interviewer marks an X on the Scale Regarding Organizational Commitment Level of Implementation)
	
	Little Partial Full
	Implementation Implementation Implementation
	1-------2-------3-------4-------5-------6-------7
		- Staff changes.
		- Room and location.
		- Organizational charge
		- Schedule.
		  Actions taken by principal.
		  A significant curriculum design change will require organizational changes.
		- Are in teachers' hands.
		- All available.
		- Learner materials or teacher materials.
		- Regular follow-ups or one shot.
		- All teachers at once or personalized and small group learning.
		- Peer support and other school linkages.
		- Inservice activities are scheduled.
		- Clinical supervision for refinement of teaching skills.

extra effort in scheduling. A few (small group) of learners can usually be collected and interviewed quietly for ten minutes or so right in the classroom with the help of the teacher in charge to fit this in appropriately with other classroom activities.

IMPLICATIONS OF THE STATE OF IMPLEMENTATION OF THE CURRICULUM FOR EVALUATION ACTIVITIES

Kohler's study of implementation levels concluded that generally the commitment level pervades all phases of the process but that the other levels, organizational, teacher roles, and learner roles generally proceed in a sequence over time. This, first and most clearly, suggests that evaluation of learner outcomes such as achievement is inappropriate until other levels of implementation are evidently in place. Other findings suggest that the staff commitment to the curriculum based on personal values of teachers is an essential. Any evaluation study undertaken without an assessment of commitment should be suspect.

Table 6 Continued

Dimension	1) Suggested Questions(s) a) Follow-up or Probe Question(s)	("Listen For" Examples)
Perceptions of Teacher Level of Implementation	1) How are the teachers doing by now? a) Have they run into any snags? b) How do they feel about it? c) Do you have some examples? (Interviewer marks an X on the Scale Regarding Institutional Commitment Level Implementation) Little Partial Full Implementation Implementation Implementation 1-------2-------3-------4-------5-------6-------7	- Is the answer vague or do you hear concrete examples which the supervisor has seen or discussed with teachers?

Timing and purpose of an evaluation study probably should follow the sequence of implementation phases. For example, a study of the staff development support component is appropriate after institutional and organizational levels of implementation are near completion. Studies of student outcomes become relevant when the teacher role level has been implemented and the learner activity level is being addressed. A final implication to be reinforced is that implementation of a curriculum design takes a great deal of time, perhaps three to five years. Efforts to evaluate a curriculum should proceed with awareness of this time frame.

SUMMARY

In this chapter the case is made that evaluation efforts must take into account the nature of the implementation of a curriculum rather than assume that it has occurred. Three research studies are reviewed which present alternative ways to evaluate the implementation levels of a curriculum. Finally, this chapter presents information and examples about how to develop and carry out an assessment of implementation of any particular curriculum design being used in a school.

Suggested Study Activities

1. Study a written description of a curriculum and analyze its design for types of learning strategies and teaching methods implied in practice.
2. Using the example protocol in the chapter interview a supervisor in your own district regarding a particular curriculum.
3. Develop an example interview protocol for use with the principal regarding a particular curriculum.

4. Study and report on the "Levels of Use" method of assessing implementation.
5. Search the ERIC resources for other potentially valuable efforts to assess curriculum implementation.

Self Assessment

1. Can you name, explain, and give examples of levels of reality of implementation of a curriculum according to Charters and Jones?
2. Can you describe and note some strengths and weaknesses of efforts to date to assess the implementation of educational programs?
3. Can you explain how to develop a plan for the assessment of the implementation of a curriculum?

References

Charters, W. W. and Jones, J. On the Risk of Appraising Non-events in Program Evaluation. *Educational Researcher,* 1973, 2 (11), 5–7.

Hall, Gene E. and Loucks, Susan A Developmental Model for Determining Whether the Treatment is Actually Implemented *American Educational Research Journal* Vol. 14, No. 3, pp. 263–276.

Halvorsen, James and Paden, Jon S. *Survey of Effective School Processes: Interview and Observation Handbook* Dayton, Ohio: I/D/E/A Inc., The Educational Affiliate of the Charles F. Kettering Foundation.

Kohler, Richard A. A Study of Commitment of Staff to Implement an Innovative Educational Program. Unpublished Doctoral Dissertation, University of Cincinnati, 1976.

Leonard, Wm. H. and Lowry, Lawrence Was There Really an Experiment?: A Quantitative Procedure for Verifying Treatments in Educational Research *Educational Researcher* Vol. 8, No. 6, pp 4–7.

Chapter 7

CURRICULUM EVALUATION BEGINS WITH A QUESTION

As a result of studying this chapter, the reader should be able to:

1. Classify questions on the basis of whether they are problem questions or solution questions.
2. Generate questions related to each of the types of decisions of curriculum evaluation.
3. Classify questions within the five components of the curriculum domain represented by the curriculum wheel paradigm.

Curriculum evaluation is the search for information to contribute to the change, improvement, or maintenance of the curriculum/instruction/learning program. It deals with areas of curriculum design, instructional means, curriculum resources, staff development, the learner experience cycle, and the developmental stages of planning, implementing, and outcomes. This search for information is based upon the statement of a concern or problem posed in the form of a question.

QUESTIONS ARISE FROM NEEDS AND CONCERNS

The background to the curriculum evaluation question may be the recognition of a need in the curriculum program. A need is defined as a gap or a discrepancy between two things which by any reasonable thought should be the same or similar but are not. To simply illustrate this gap, the school district average for daily attendance of pupils might be 91 percent, while the daily attendance for a single school might be 82 percent. It is reasonable to assume that daily attendance expressed by these two numbers should be reasonably alike and is not. The question is easily formed, "What factors are contributing to the low daily attendance of pupils?"

The second definition of a need is a gap or discrepancy between a real state of affairs and an ideal state of affairs. To illustrate with the attendance example, it might be shown that absence due to illness is irreducible below 3 percent of a school population of 600 or less pupils. If, then, the ideal state of daily attendance is 97 percent, we may not be comparing a school to a district average, but a school and district to an "ideal" percent of daily attendance when we ask, "What are the factors which contribute to the low daily attendance within the school district?

The background for stating an evaluation question may be an expression of a concern or a perceived need instead of a quantifiable gap as the example of pupil attendance suggested. A concern may be raised by a question such as, "Is the math curriculum effective? Are we putting too much time into one area or another?"

A CURRICULUM EVALUATION QUESTION MUST HAVE A QUALITY OF OPENNESS

The first caution in stating or forming the question of the curriculum evaluation plan is to be sure the question is a problem and not a symptom. For example, "Are we wasting time?" may mean that the priorities are changing or are unclear. A symptom question often expresses a particular condition that is dependent on a problem. Time, for example, never seems wasted when one is doing something important. So the question of wasting time may really be a question of priorities.

SYMPTOM QUESTIONS ARE INDIRECT AND OFF TARGET

The second caution in stating or forming the question is to avoid fantasies. Fantasies are offered as simplistic answers to the question. Fantasies are really opinions offered from the *Everybody Knows* body of knowledge, and they are often accepted without much reaction. For example, "Most of our parents feel this way or that," when no one really knows, is a fantasy. Fantasy denies the commitment and need to seek information.

Avoid solution questions. A solution question is one which already contains its answer. For example, "How can we insure that every student is reading at the 11th grade level as measured by the national surveys?" (Kinghorn, 1974) is a solution question. It suggests that all we need is information about ways to do it. Such a closed question is an outcome already identified. It specifies the change required and so heightens the possible defensive reactions. Curriculum evaluation questions should be stated as problem questions not solution questions. The problem question will have a quality of openness about it which will allow the people involved to commit themselves to a search for information, and to the information and derive meanings for appropriate actions and changes.

In summary, the development of the curriculum evaluation question should be the expression of a problem. It should have a quality of openness about it which would permit the people involved to follow the principles of feedback in seeking information, interpreting that information, and making decisions regarding change and improvement of curriculum programs.

TYPES OF DECISIONS AND THE CURRICULUM EVALUATION QUESTION

Curriculum Evaluation questions begin the feedback process of providing information by which we may make choices about stability, change, and growth. These choices have been described as four types of decisions by Stufflebeam (1971).

Planning decisions have to do with what is intended as outcomes of the curriculum program, what we should do and why. The following are questions which are relatable to planning decisions:

1. What should be the goals of the curriculum or program?
2. What goals should have priority?
3. What needs of community, society, and learner are to be served by this curriculum or program?
4. What knowledge is most important to learn?
5. What should be the outcomes of the curriculum?
6. What should we expect of graduates?
7. What values are most important to preserve or influence through the program?
8. For what outcomes should we be educating in the future?
9. Are we up-to-date in our present goals and expectations for this curriculum or learning program?

A second type of decision which educators face is the structuring decision according to Stufflebeam (1971). This could just as well be called the *designing* decision as it pertains to designing of procedures to accomplish the ends identified by planning decisions. This is the "How should we do it?" question. We are concerned with what designs, what curricula, what resources, what methods, what organization, what schedule, what curricular materials will be chosen. Some example questions which relate to Design or Structuring decisions are:

1. What textbook would best support a process approach in science?
2. What scheduling procedures would be consistent with a true middle school concept?
3. What do our teachers need to know or be able to do to implement this kind of curriculum?
4. Are these materials suitable for our learners?
5. Does the district philosophy statement support the middle school design?
6. Should we choose open space or traditional classroom organization?
7. What is the optimum class size?
8. What are the effective uses of lecturing, small group methods, inquiry method, etc.?

Implementing decisions (Stufflebeam, 1971) are those choices we must make when we put the curriculum into action. The evaluation question which relates to implementing decisions is, "Are we doing it?" These are questions about the effectiveness of what is occurring. This is sometimes referred to as the process phase. We are interested in this phase in the use we are making of the curriculum design, the fidelity with which we are working, the consequences of our actions, and the *uncontrollable influences* with which we are confronted.

Example questions which relate to implementing decisions are:

1. Are we following the curriculum which we agreed to?
2. Is this program working?
3. What do we do with students who aren't ready for this?
4. How many program levels can be managed in one classroom?
5. Could we have an inservice session?
6. What kinds of questioning strategies fit this curriculum?
7. What do the parents think?
8. What do the learners understand about small group learning?
9. Do the learners understand the purpose of the program, lesson, unit?

Recycling decisions (Stufflebeam, 1971) are those choices we make based upon our knowledge of results and attainments. These decisions relate to changing or maintaining the curriculum. The question which best relates to the recycling decision is, "Did we do it?" Some examples of this question are:

1. What are the results of the learning program?
2. What are our graduates like?
3. How do we really know what the learners have learned?
4. What parts of the curriculum had priority?
5. What did we leave out?
6. Are our graduates competent?
7. Which parts of the curriculum have been relevant to our graduates?
8. Have we accomplished our objectives?
9. Is this an effective learning program?

The four generic questions which relate to decisions of planning, designing, implementing, and recycling are:

1. What should we do?
2. How should we do it?
3. Are we doing it?
4. Did we do it?

These questions are very similar to the four questions which must be answered in development of any curriculum plan according to Tyler (1949). In this relation we find that curriculum evaluation is not far removed from curriculum planning. In curriculum planning we seek to create the potential for a learner's experience. In curriculum evaluation we seek information which will provide new meaning out of our experiences with the learning program and curriculum plan, and through those new meanings we can renew, improve, and maintain a significant learning program.

COMPONENTS OF THE CURRICULUM DOMAIN AND THE CURRICULUM EVALUATION QUESTION

Five interacting components, Figure 4, make up the Curriculum Domain: Curriculum Design, Instructional Means, Resources, Staff Development, and the Learner Experience Cycle. The three stages are: Planning, Implementing, and Outcomes.

In clarifying or stating the question which initiates the curriculum evaluation plan, it may be useful to identify in which component of the

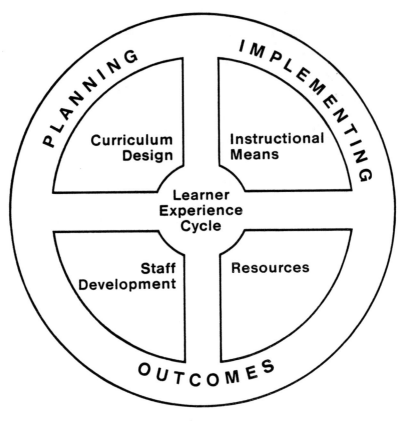

Figure 4
Curriculum Domain

curriculum domain this question is found and whether it is a question which relates to the stage of planning, implementing, or outcomes. This exercise in classifying the question can help us to state the question with more precision and to suggest the variables from which we will get the information and perhaps give an early hint about methods of information gathering.

As example, questions are stated here to illustrate the components and stages of curriculum domain, it is important to remember that the components and stages are used to identify fluid and dynamic areas. None of these components or stages are static or neatly bounded and separable from the others. Therefore, the example questions are illustrative, but not exclusive to a single part of the curriculum domain.

Let us begin with a curriculum evaluation question such as, "What is the personal experience and attitude of our learners as they engage in inquiry activities in science?" This question focuses the evaluation on the center of the curriculum wheel; in Figure 4, *the learner experience cycle.* The state of the question implies that it is an implementing stage. If it were a planning stage of the learner experience cycle, we might have asked, "What are the conditions of readiness for a learner to engage in inquiry activities?" If the concern were at an outcomes stage, we might have asked, "What is the transferability of inquiry processes which our learners have experienced in classroom activities?"

In the resource component, we might ask, "What operational criteria could be used to select a curricular material which would be 'good' for inquiry activities?" This question is posed in the planning stage of resourcing. "Which of our textbooks was most effective for inquiry activities?" suggests a test of their use and may therefore be an outcomes stage of the resources used. The implementing stage of resourcing may overlap considerably with instructional strategies and methods when we pose the question, "Can any material be used to generate inquiry processes by the learner?"

In the component of staff development we are concerned with growth, development, knowledge, and skill of the teacher related to the curriculum. At the planning stage we might pose the question, "What are the inservice needs of teachers regarding the inquiry curriculum?" At the implementation stage we might ask, "Are our inservice sessions consistent with what we expect teachers to be able to do in the classroom?" At the outcomes stage of the staff development component, we might ask, "What performance behaviors of teachers in the classroom are identifiable as a result of the inservice on inquiry?"

In the component of Instructional Means at the planning stage we might ask, "Are there different lesson planning techniques which are effective for inquiry units and class sessions?" At the implementing stage we might ask, "What sequence of learning activities in the class session seems to facilitate inquiry?" At the outcomes stage we might ask, "How can the teacher know if inquiry processes have taken place?"

In the component of Curriculum Design at the planning stage we might ask, "What are the needs of learners in today's society for inquiry skills?" At the implementation stage of Curriculum Design we might ask, "What priority do the board, the teachers, and the parents give to inquiry as a curriculum goal for the school?" At the outcomes stage of Curriculum Design we might ask, "Does the Curriculum Inquiry Design chosen fit the principles and philosophy statement of the school board's adopted resolution on the goals and mission of the school district?"

These example questions have been offered to show that it is possible to think of and pose curriculum evaluation questions in each of the five components of the curriculum domain and within each component to be concerned primarily with the curriculum development stage of planning or implementing or outcomes. It is not necessary to pose your curriculum evaluating question in this way. It may be useful once the problem has been stated to think about it in these terms for further clarification or in anticipation of the kinds of targets or variables you will need to consider when you gather information.

SUMMARY

Stating the question begins the curriculum evaluation plan. The quality of openness of the question in terms of whether it addresses a problem or a solution hidden in the question often affects how or whether the people involved can deal with it. If evaluation is intended to supply information for decision making, it will be helpful to identify the evaluation question with one of the four types of decisions: planning, structuring, implementing, or recycling. It may also be useful to examine or classify the question in terms of the five curriculum domain components, learner experience cycle, resources, staff development, instructional means, and curriculum design.

Suggested Activities

1. Interview a school principal, supervisor, or department leader on the subject of important questions about curriculum, instruction, and learning. Classify the questions according to the components of the curriculum wheel. Share the diagram of the curriculum wheel during your interview to see if the relationship of the five components to the questions can be helpfully discussed.
2. Read an evaluation report and attempt to identify the evaluation question which guided the study. You may be able to verify your opinion by communicating with the author of the report.
3. Write a curriculum question for each area of the curriculum wheel which relates to the basic skills phase of curriculum design.

Self-Assessment

1. Can you pose a solution type question and then revise so that it becomes a problem type question?
2. Can you give one example question related to:
   a. Planning decisions?
   b. Designing decisions?
   c. Implementing decisions?
   d. Recycling decisions?
3. Can you take a curriculum evaluation question and categorize it using the Curriculum Wheel?

References

Kinghorn, John R. We Agree Workshop for Small-Group Leaders Plus Two Additional Group Skill Activities, I/D/E/A Staff Paper, Dayton, Ohio: Institute for Development of Educational Activities, Inc., August 1974.

Stufflebeam, Daniel L., et al. *Educational Evaluation and Decision Making,* Phi Delta Kappa National Study Committee on Evaluation. Itasca, Illinois: F. E. Peacock Publishers, 1971, pp. 79–84.

Tyler, Ralph W. *Basic Principles of Curriculum and Instruction,* Chicago: University of Chicago Press: 1949, p. 1.

Chapter 8

DEVELOPING THE EVALUATION PLAN: WHAT QUESTION? WHAT INFORMATION? FROM WHOM? HOW?

As a result of this chapter, the reader should be able to:

1. Define and use appropriately the terms: concepts, variables, operational, and instrumental definitions of variables.
2. Outline the steps of a process to develop a curriculum evaluation plan which includes a curriculum question, subquestions, evidence needed, source, and method of gathering information.
3. Perform an analysis process which begins with a curriculum question and leads to a completed evaluation planning chart.

S tating the curriculum evaluation question is the critical, first step in the development of an evaluation plan. This question would best come from a dialogue or consensus process of the people involved with the curriculum, including teachers, administrators, and supervisors, with input from such others as board members, parents, and learners. Given this involvement and investment in creating the question, the first condition of evaluation as feedback has been met. Namely, that feedback is sought after information. The next step after setting the general question is to give the evaluation process clear focus. Evaluation as feedback deals with specific information. To retrieve specific information in an evaluation, we must identify which variables must be observed.

Variables refer to properties of ideas or concepts which may be operationalized by definitions so that measures of perceptions can be taken from the real setting and used as information for feedback. It is the next task to review the steps necessary to get from the curriculum evaluation question (the general idea) to the specific questions suggesting those observable and measurable qualities (variables) which are the true focus of the evaluation plan.

THE CURRICULUM EVALUATION PLANNING CHART

Before proceeding through an example, a brief overview of an evaluation planning chart would help to keep the steps in mind. Figure 5 provides five major categories which must be decided in any plan. Stage one is the general curriculum question chosen or identified with the concerned persons. It is the assumption here that this involvement is critical to making meaning of the later feedback of information and effecting any sort of change in behavior of the persons who have charge of the program.

Stage two of the figure is the specification of questions implied in the general question. This focusing of the main question from column one involves several analysis activities which are best done by the persons involved in the curriculum. Column three is titled *Evidence Needed.* In the example to follow, several activities are suggested for getting to the operational definitions of variables which will give evidence that truly relates to each sub-question. The *Source of Evidence* category should identify the person, group, or data source from which the evidence can be gathered, such as student, parent, teacher, employer, administrator, 3rd graders, etc.

Stage five of the chart provides the decision as to how the evidence can be gathered. In both column four and five, the planners may wish to corroborate the information by using more than one source, for example, reading behavior at home could be sought from students and parents. Or regarding methods, we might give a reading interest inventory to students and we might observe behaviors of students at a book fair or in the library to corroborate interest.

The Curriculum Evaluation Planning Chart is an excellent tool for mapping out the actual plan of an evaluation. A group process for developing each step of the plan is described in the following example. The planning chart can be used by an individual evaluator to think through a project. It can also be filled in out-of-order just as the thoughts or ideas become clear in planning. When completed, a curriculum evaluation planning chart can be used to set out the schedule of when evidence will be gathered, by whom, and where. This valuable tool can be the central map by which an evaluation is planned and managed.

What Is Our Concern?	What do We Really Want to Know?		Where Can We Find Out?	How Can We Find Out?
General Curriculum Evaluation Question	Sub-Questions	Evidence Needed	Source of the Evidence	Methods and Instruments

Figure 5
Curriculum Evaluation Planning Chart

A GROUP PROCESS EXAMPLE OF EVALUATION PLANNING

The initial step, Table 7, is the written form of a general curriculum evaluation question. In this example we have chosen the question, "Has reading improved?" It is a realistic concern, typically expressed by language arts teachers, parents, or principals in many schools. The emphasis in Step 1 is that all parties who have a stake in making the program go have had a say in the formation of this question, and will have some part in getting to the specific sub-questions which explain what they mean. This involvement is one condition for making meaning of information in the final stages of the evaluation.

Formulating this question in Table 7 concludes the first step completed in the planning chart. To get to step 2 in the planning chart, the specific questions, we must proceed with several group process activities to analyze, critique, and prioritize the meanings people have about the original question. The first of these activities is the brainstorming of a list of the possible subquestions which express the variables that the program people mean by reading improvement.

Table 7
Example: Posing the Curriculum Evaluation Question

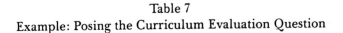

Has Reading Improved?

Persons involved in this activity should be brought together for a working session which will include brainstorming, critiquing, prioritizing, and validation. The rules of brainstorming should be reviewed: Keep to the specific issue of reading improvement. Generate as many ideas as possible. No evaluative judgments or criticism of anyone's proposal is allowed at this point. Piggy-backing one idea from someone else's is encouraged. A recorder and time-keeper should be identified within the group to write down and number suggestions on a large paper or chalk-board for all to see. It may be useful for the group recorder to offer an example as the first of the brainstormed list. In this example, Table 8, the trigger or example subquestion was "1. Can students read faster?" This example may help the group keep in mind that the general question dealt with improvement over something, a comparison. The purpose of brainstorming this list is to get identified all possible notions of the variables which may be assumed or implied by the people who generated the original curriculum evaluation question. It is appropriate to have other resource persons such as experts in reading join in the brainstorming process.

There are several more activities necessary in the group process before a final list of subquestions can be entered into column two of the evaluation planning chart, Figure 5. The next step is for the working group to

Table 8
Example: Brainstormed List of Sub-Questions

```
 *1.  Can students read faster?
  2.  Do students decode more accurately?
  3.  Is there more use of the library?
  4.  Have comprehension skills increased?
  5.  Are reading grades better?
  6.  Do students enjoy reading more?
  7.  Do students read in their spare time?
  8.  Has reading performance improved in content area?
  9.  Has fluency improved?
 10.  Has vocabulary expanded?
 11.  Are children selecting higher level reading?
 12.  How many books have students read?
 13.  Have IQ scores risen?
 14.  Have inquiry skills improved?
 15.  Have attitudes, behavior, and attendance changed?
 16.  Has TV viewing time at home decreased?
 17.  Are students more interested in reading?

 *Starting question as illustration
```

review their brainstormed list and to eliminate unclear thinking. Any questions found on the list which are broad and general, and do not point rather directly to some observable and/or measurable quality of reading as it improves, should be separately discussed and restated, or brainstormed for specific meanings, or eliminated. Questions in the brainstormed list, Table 8 like number 17, "Are students more interested in reading?" could be clarified or brainstormed to determine what is meant by interest, how could it be observed. A question like "13. Have IQ scores risen?" should be challenged for meaning. Is it, after all, an observable and measurable variable that reflects reading improvement? What was the suggestion meant to specify about reading improvement. Duplicate subquestions, if any, should be eliminated at this time. Each question in the list should be examined in this way to cull out the duplicates, the remotely related ones, to restate or make specific the vague or too general subquestions which don't offer much notion of the observable variables which the subquestion should address. This may also be a time for adding a question which seems to have been missed in the first effort to generate the list. Table 9 is an example of how the critiqued list of subquestions might now appear.

Table 9
Example: Critiqued List of Sub-Questions

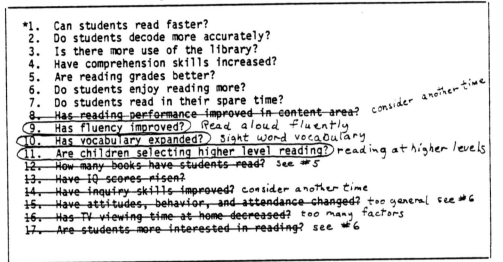

The next step for the working group would be to prioritize a final list of subquestions to enter onto the evaluation planning chart, Figure 5. This can be done in several ways. One useful examination of the subquestions is to describe categories into which the questions could be classified. For example, the list in Table 9 might be classified by such categories as: attitude and interest in reading, reading skills, achievement, or outcomes of reading. This analysis by classification can assist the work group to understand the practical definition which they have been applying to the original question. The work group may also rate each subquestion by placing an E or H by the question on the sheet according to the following:

How hard (time consuming/expensive) would it be to get a complete answer to this question?

very easy   E
very hard   H

Then each subquestion can be discussed and rated by the following criteria:

If we had a complete answer to this single sub-question alone, could we say whether reading has improved?

yes   —   Y
no   —   N

The optimum outcome of this critique would be that we identify a limited number of the subquestions which seem to be easy to get an answer to, and which we agree would tell us whether reading had improved. Table 10 is an example of what the list of subquestions might look like following the prioritizing activity. The answers to the critiquing and prioritizing activities of the work group are subject to the values, expertise, and choices of the members. Another work group might have come to somewhat different conclusions. We should make sure in constituting its membership that the group contains the perspective and resources to make these analyses and decisions.

Table 10
Example: Prioritized List of Sub-Questions

```
Attitude Toward Reading Category

3.   Is there more use of the library?
6.   Do students enjoy reading more?
7.   Do students read in their spare time?

Reading Skills Category

1.   Can students read faster?
2.   Do students decode more accurately?
3.   Have comprehension skills increased?
9.   Read aloud fluently?

Achievement in Reading

5.   Are reading grades better?
10.  Increased sight word vocabulary?
11.  Reading at higher levels?
```

One final discussion of the work group about the subquestions remains before entering them into the evaluation planning chart. The validation of the subquestions flows from the following question: If we had answers to these prioritized subquestions, would we be able to determine whether reading had improved? If the work group can reply "Yes" to this question, the subquestions can be entered onto the second column of the planning chart. This may also be a time to ask other groups such as teachers or supervisors to validate the questions as well using the same question.

DETERMINING THE EVIDENCE NEEDED

The third step on the evaluation planning chart is to identify the variable(s). This means to define the ideas within each subquestion in terms of the things observable or measurable.

Concepts are abstract; they exist only as ideas. Variables are the aspect or cue of an idea which can be translated into observable or measurable definitions (Kerlinger, 1973). These definitions suggest what to look for and often how to look at the real situation.

There are two important characteristics of variables to introduce now which will be important to the evaluation process as it develops. First, the measurable variable of a concept (idea) should never be treated as the idea itself. Such a slip in thinking can lead to very rigid decision making. For instance, intelligence is an idea, while I.Q. is a measured variable from which we infer or conjecture about some aspects of intelligence. Interchanging a measure for the larger idea itself is sloppy thinking, which can lead to unprofessional kinds of decision making. Second, variables have different tendencies to change (vary). This will suggest how we measure them a little later in the evaluation plan. Blood type, for instance, varies not at all within a single case. Height varies slowly over time. Fatigue varies quickly and in regular cycles. Likewise, measuring motivation should be thought of over time, while measuring a variable like interest may have short time changes.

Variables refer to properties of ideas (concepts) which may be operationalized by definitions so that perceptions or measures can be taken of the real setting and used as information for creating feedback and making meaning. An operational definition describes the concrete things or events which can be observed or corrected. For example, class participation could be defined as the number of times a child raises his/her hand during a class discussion. A second form of definition is referred to as an instrumental definition because the variable is defined as a score on a known test device. An example of an instrumental definition of the concept of reading achievement could be the total reading score on the Stanford Achievement Test in Language Arts.

Stating an operational definition for each subquestion is quite similar to developing behavioral forms of objectives. In this approach Mager (1972) provided some very interesting strategies. A helpful way to begin is to have the evaluation planning work group think of what a student who had improved in reading would say or do regarding each of these questions. An obverse way to think about the same issue would be to imagine what a student who had not yet improved in reading would not yet be able to do. A third strategy Mager suggested to operationally define each subquestion would be to imagine a room full of students which must be divided into two groups, those who had improved on each subquestion and those who had not. A list of the cues or attributes which one might use to separate the group can be helpful in creating an operational definition. It may also be clear to the work group that a test instrument is available or in use at the school which can provide a score regarding the subquestion.

To consider example subquestions 1 and 2 from Table 9 we must remember that the overall question is about improvement, and these questions suggest comparison... *read faster,... more accurately.* Obviously, when we consider the method of measurement, a baseline or previous measure from the past will be necessary.

Question 1, "Can students read faster?" can be operationally defined as reading silently paragraphs or passages from their reading book. The definition can include words per minute as the definition of reading rate. The operational definition can also contain conditions or givens much like a behavioral objective. For example, given an unfamiliar story in the students regular level reading series, more students (a percentage may be useful) will complete the passage reading silently in the allotted time than were able to do so at the beginning of the school year, or as compared to groups not in this particular reading program, or as were able to last year at this time.

Other means to measure speed and accuracy could be defined instrumentally as scores on a standardized test of reading. Teacher-made tests are also appropriate as instrumental definitions and as was pointed out in the discussion of issues, such tests often reflect more validly than purchased tests what the instructional curriculum actually is.

Once the operational definitions are stated, they should be checked to see that they contain clarity of conditions, behaviors to be observed or measured, and criteria or levels of performance. If the work group has agreed on this review, the operational definitions are valid. External resource persons can also be used in the validation process. The operational or instrumental definitions can now be entered or paraphrased and entered onto the evaluation planning chart.

SOURCE OF THE EVIDENCE

The column of the planning chart (Figure 5) titled Source of the Evidence refers to the person or subject of the observation such as the students in the "Ultrabrite Reading Program," or all class of 4th and 7th grade students. It might also refer to parents or teachers, if a survey instrument involved them. We could also consider sources of the students' work or effort in this column such as student records, student project work, student notebooks, etc.

METHODS AND INSTRUMENTS

The methods and instruments column of the evaluation planning chart provides a place to record unobtrusive measures like book wear and page wear, informal measures such as observing library behavior of students, formal or structured measures like classroom observation checklists, and test instruments.

As the planning chart is completed, the work group should consider at least two different methods for measuring or observing each variable. One method could be formal and the other informal. This provides certain validity to the findings as one method serves to check on the other. It also may provide two different kinds of answers to the subquestion, one a results answer and the other an interpretive answer. For example, a standardized test on reading speed and comprehension can provide quantitative information in percentages about the students' behavior, while an observation of silent reading time in the classroom can reveal subtleties about reading rate and fatigue, interest, times of day, and types of literature. Both kinds of information are necessary to validate and interpret reading behavior of students. Either kind of information alone is rather incomplete and lacking for potential meaning making by the professional staff.

SUMMARY

The Curriculum Evaluation Planning Chart is a very useful tool for developing a complete evaluation through the five steps: general curriculum evaluation question, subquestions, evidence needed, source of evidence, and methods and instruments needed. A working group process which involves the curriculum implementors can be used to prepare the evaluation plan. This involvement of people and the focusing of the evaluation from a common concern to the operational definitions of the variables and the methods for gathering information is essential to the concept of feedback. The making of meaning for curriculum improvement is the true definition of curriculum evaluation proposed by this plan.

Suggested Activities

1. Using a planning chart, interview a teacher for approximately 30 minutes and develop a curriculum evaluation planning chart around a single relevant question.
2. Volunteer to lead a work group in the preparation of a curriculum evaluation planning chart for your department or school curriculum committee.
3. Explain the concept and steps for developing a curriculum evaluation planning chart at your next faculty meeting. Prepare and use overhead transparencies or wall charts and keep your presentation to a 20 minute agenda time.

Self Assessment

1. Can you define these terms?
   a. Concept
   b. Variable
   c. Operational definition
   d. Instrumental definition
2. Can you list in sequence the group work steps suggested in the chapter to move from a general curriculum evaluation question to subquestions?
3. Can you list suggested steps in sequence for taking a sub-question and developing an operational or instrumental definition of the variable?
4. Can you take a concern or evaluation question from your own professional experience and develop a complete curriculum evaluation planning chart for it?

References

Kerlinger, Fred H. *Foundations of Behavioral Research* 2nd Edition. New York: Holt, Rinehart and Winston, 1973.

Mager, Robert F. *Goal Analysis* Belmont, California: Fearon Publishers, 1972.

Chapter 9

SAMPLING AND DESIGN

As a result of this chapter, the reader should be able to:

1. Define and describe the purposes of random sampling in curriculum evaluation.
2. Select a random sample using a table of random numbers and a five step technique.
3. Determine a sample size from a finite population with a 95 percent confidence of falling within .2 standard deviation of the population mean.
4. Describe the most common errors of sampling which can distort the findings of an evaluation study.
5. Describe the nature and uses of a a-experimental, experimental, and quasi experimental designs for curriculum evaluation studies.

"It's not necessary to drink an entire quart of milk to find out if it's sour or sweet."

Popham

Sampling is a valuable every day technique in life. For example, from a very small sample of blood of an individual, a diagnosis can be made of the state of health of the whole person. From a vial of water, chemists can determine the presence of organisms and pollutants in the water supply of an entire city. The cook takes just one added step by stirring the pot of soup before tasting a spoonful to be sure it has just the right flavor. The stirring before sipping helps assure that every ingredient in the pot is represented in the single spoonful. Sampling in the physical world works very well because processes like diffusion help to distribute things evenly or randomly throughout.

In human events and social settings, we live and act based upon experience sampling. When visiting a school, for instance, we gain an overall impression of the school by asking: the principal what his or her goals for the school year are; a teacher what are highlights of the year so far; and a student why they are studying a particular lesson. We notice whether the artwork hanging on the walls is commercial, teacher made, or student made. We notice the colors, sounds and activities of people, the mail boxes in the office, and dozens of other things. From these experience samples we may conclude that this school is a good school, a hard-working school, a warm and personable school, or perhaps an innovative school.

Such experience sampling can be used in tentative ways or in rigid ways. It may take into consideration the best we know from research and experience and the *grain-of-salt* notion that whatever you see or hear cannot be the whole story. Or a person may be dissuaded by a single cue or in fact have fulfilled a bias or prejudice such as having heard that a school was poor or outstanding and sure enough finding it so. This effect of expectations has been substantiated in research on teaching (Rosenthal, 1968).

One task of the classroom teacher is the continuous sampling of student behavior. During diagnosis, sampling of student behaviors helps to understand prior learnings, entry level skills, learning styles and preferences, interests, and attitudes. Sampling of student behaviors occurs in monitoring student progress, in adjusting or revising the teaching strategies and learning environments to the emerging learner needs, and in the outcome measurement of student achievements. Sampling of both a formal and informal nature is a central professional task of teachers.

The examples of experience sampling serve here to illustrate that not only is it an everyday, or perhaps every moment occurrence, but that it follows a process of evaluation and meaning making which is similar to our basis for curriculum evaluation. A sample of situations, events, or behaviors are sought through any of a number of different ways. *The impressions from these samples are interpreted using our past experience, previous samples, knowledge and research of others, and our value and belief system to make meaning.* The meaning restructures what we understand and value to the extent that it confirms, adjusts, or changes the meanings we hold. From this basis we are prepared to act, to seek new experience samples, and to grow.

RANDOM SAMPLING

Random sampling is a technique akin to stirring the soup before drawing out one spoonful to taste. In sampling from a large population of students, for instance, we want to accomplish two things: first, that what we find out about the sample is very reasonably like what the whole population of students would have been; and second, that no particular bias (to which we may not have given much thought) such as early risers or big breakfast eaters, will be found concentrated in the sample. Random sampling reasonably assures that all biases, whether we have considered them or not, are distributed in the sample in about the same way they are found in the whole population.

Random sampling is a process of selecting a sample which ensures that every member of the population had an equally likely chance to be in the sample. This represents one use of random sampling, to select a sample so that results from the sample represent the whole population. The second use of randomizing is to assign subjects to treatments in an experimental-control study so that whatever biases there are, from summer birthdays to big breakfast eaters, may not influence one part of the study any more or less than other parts of the study or bias an experimental treatment group any differently than a control group.

Stratified random sampling is a special type of sampling to ensure that definite kinds or categories of subjects are known to be in the sample. For example, random sampling by grade level is a type of stratified process that will ensure that we can examine the effects of an evaluation study which represents each grade level of the school. Some stratification categories often considered to account for bias in curriculum evaluation studies are age and cognitive development, sex, ethnic background, and vocational preference.

Matrix sampling is a specialized form of random sampling which can be used to assign certain items of a survey, for example, to randomly selected samples of people from a very large population. This technique permits the breaking down of a very large number of items in a survey so that no single subject is burdened with a long and fatiguing experience answering the survey.

Most of the sampling done in curriculum evaluation studies is used in content analysis of texts and curricular materials, classroom observation of environmental conditions or student and teacher behaviors, individual student progress, classrooms as units in a district or multiple district study, parent surveys, and community surveys.

TECHNIQUES FOR RANDOM SAMPLING

One of the least complicated approaches to random selection is the use of slips of paper shaken around in a bowl. It is subject to errors of mixing, bent and unequal paper slips, and so on. It is also true that such a method could be very laborious with large numbers and time consuming, and not recommended for its practical elimination of bias.

A second very practical approach for random assignment which might be used quite appropriately in a class or grade level sized evaluation study would be the use of a regular deck of playing cards to generate the random selection.

A pack of playing cards thoroughly shuffled are subject to $80,658 \times 10$ possible ordered sequences of the 52 cards. For practical purposes, such a mathematic potential can be considered equivalent to a random series. With a list of names of students in a reasonably small population, the deck of cards may be used to assign students to two treatment groups (black cards versus red cards), or to four treatment groups (four suits of the pack), or to a limited sample of the group (face cards only). For sampling from a population of more than the number of cards in the pack, it is necessary only to return to the beginning of the pack and continue to draw in its established sequence.

The best approach is to use a table of random numbers (see Appendix B). The table of random numbers is a table of the digits 0 through 9 which appear continuously in random order.

The following steps will create a random sample from a population:

1. Make a complete list of all subjects in the population and number the list (class attendance lists are useful).
2. Group digits in the random table in pairs or triads so that they represent the size of the numerals used in the total population. For instance, 99 or less persons can be represented by pairs of digits (04, 23, 89, etc.) or 100 through 999 persons in a population can be represented by three digits combined in the table (043, 235, etc.).
3. Choose a starting place on the table and proceed down the columns or across the rows in a consistent way. For example, you may choose someone's birthday, month and date, as a key to a beginning spot. For instance, the sixth column from the left (June), the thirteenth number down the column (June 13), and proceed with pairs of digits down the columns continuously to the bottom, and then move to the left top of the next column.

4. Skip numbers as you go through the random number table which exceed your population size or are duplicates of numbers you already have selected. For instance, if you have 250 students in the population, all three digit numbers over 250 are ignored. And, if number 048 has been selected once, ignore the number if it comes up again in the table.
5. Continue selecting numbers which coincide with the list until the sample size wanted has been completed.

DETERMINING SAMPLE SIZE

The basic guideline for sample size is that one wants to be confident that the average of the sample for any variable is very near the average of the whole population from which the sample was drawn. Up to a point, the larger the sample chosen, the closer the mean of the sample will be to the mean of the population. A fair rule of thumb is that if you have a random sample of at least thirty, and this number is ten percent or more of the total population, the possible error will be small.

Gottman and Clasen (1972) have proposed a simplified statistical procedure for deciding what size sample to choose. For a population of known size (for example, a grade level of 300 students), the following formula for determining sample size is suggested:

n = sample size
N = total population
D = proportion of standard deviation from the population mean which we wish to hold the sample within.

$$n \geq \frac{N}{ND^2 + 1}$$

If the population is 300 subjects, and we could be satisfied that the sample average would fall closer than .2 of a standard deviation from that of the population average 95 out of 100 times, the formula suggests a sample of 24:

$$n \geq \frac{300}{300(.2)^2 + 1}$$
$$n \frac{300}{13}$$
$$n \geq 24$$

Increasing the sample size to at least 30 (10 percent of the total population) or even more will decrease further the probable deviation between the sample average and that of the population.

For very large or unknown sized populations such as community populations, another approach is suggested by Gottman and Clasen for determining sample size. Using the same probability level (95 out of 100 times), a z number of 1.96 is used. A decimal amount of deviation from the population mean is chosen as tolerable error. Point two tenths (.2) was used in the last example. The z number is divided by that decimal and the quotient is then squared. A number larger than this result can be used as a sample size with the confidence that 95 out of 100 times the average of the sample will be within .2 standard deviation of the population mean. Using the above numbers, the result would lead to a sample size of 97.

$$\frac{1.96}{.2} = 9.8$$

$$9.8^2 = 96.04$$

$$97 > 96.04$$

PROBLEMS WITH SAMPLING

Several errors in selecting a sample can result in eventual distortions of an evaluation study. First, the way the sample is selected may not be truly random. For instance, having each teacher of a grade level select four students *at random* is very likely to introduce teacher bias, because at random may be four volunteers, or the first four students entering the room at first bell, or four students whose seats are central to the teacher's line of vision. Second, the whole population may be incomplete. A school with large transient population may be missing a large percentage of its grade level students by mid-year. Third, an unclear definition may lead to error. For example, in the same school of transient student population, do tenth graders who have moved into the school late in the school year still qualify by our assumptions for the evaluation study or not? Or as another illustration, do twelve years olds mean only those of one grade level, or only after a certain date? Such errors in sampling are one source of bias which can confound or distort the findings of a study.

Another concern of sampling for an evaluation study is the reality of school practice and organization. There are ethical considerations, problems of the constraints of routines, and the nature of the classroom as the organizational unit for delivery of instruction.

Ethical concern about an evaluation study may be whether the study itself intrudes upon vital time for learning. A second concern is the notion that, if one approach to learning is judged to be better, students selectively assigned to other treatments may have been short-changed. A political as well as ethical concern is whether students can be *used* in such endeavors to determine better methods of instruction.

Routines in the school may include bus transportation, school calendars, and schedules of course offerings. Random selection of students to one course or another may be resisted for many reasons by managers. It may also be true that routines once established in a school take on the quality of a cultural norm and so are very difficult to adjust.

Finally, the classroom as a unit of instruction may be the institutional component most limiting random selection of students to treatments. The case described in Chapter 15 illustrates an evaluation conducted of treatments within the class which may be a successful design.

DESIGNING CURRICULUM EVALUATION STUDIES

Research designs are a useful subject to consider when planning a curriculum evaluation. Campbell and Stanley (1963) offer a definitive description of three classes of designs, the a-experimental, the experimental, and the quasi-experimental forms of study. The use of these can suggest what situations can best be served by each, what kind of sampling will be necessary, what sort of testing and analysis may be suitable, and how rigorous the study undertaken can be.

STANDARD RESEARCH DESIGNS

A study which involves only one group with no alternative or control group is referred to as a one-shot case study. (Campbell, 1963) This may be a curriculum which everyone is required to take so there is nothing with which to compare it. Such a study may use only posttests to assess the behavior of students. This is usually the situation when the program is started without an evaluation plan in mind, or when the assumption is made that all students are beginning something new and have no real background to be assessed at the start.

A more sophisticated approach would be a case study evaluation which has a pretest and posttest assessment plan before and after the curricular experience to determine how much student behaviors change during the treatment. Such a design would only be possible if the student behaviors of consequence to the program had been identified. The dilemma in such an approach is that the program or our understanding of it changes from beginning to end, and the attention to pre and post attributes decided prior to the program implementation may be rigid and limiting.

A third, still more complex design, is known as the time series or repeated measures design (Campbell, 1963, Gottman, 1973). This design may involve a preassessment and a sampling of student behaviors at intervals throughout the program until the postassessment. Such a design allows for assessing the impact of the curriculum throughout its implementation.

Experimental designs include a control group component. This design uses random assignment to distribute the sources of variables which might aid or confound the effects among treatment groups and control groups. These conditions of random assignment and control group are very difficult to achieve in the practical setting of the school for reasons of scheduling problems, classroom instructional units, and the ethics of withholding a curricular treatment from a control group.

One critical time when effort should be made to achieve an experimental control group design for curriculum evaluation is when a quality program comes to be viewed with great skepticism by a faction within the school or community. The nature of such an objective design can be very beneficial.

There are several levels of comparison in evaluation studies which may be considered for experimental control group designs.

The first type of experimental control group comparison in curriculum has to do with comparing one curriculum with another. For example, a clear illustration from the curriculum movement of the 60's would be a comparison of a modern mathematics program with a basic or computational mathematics program. This approach is often akin to comparing apples and oranges as we discussed in Chapter 3. If such an experimental study can be organized, there must be a clear identification of the objectives or outcomes which are common to the two programs and are equally emphasized. These are the only appropriate grounds for comparison. Other benefits unique to each program should be assessed, but, of course, cannot be compared.

Experimental design can also be applied to the same curriculum which is given different emphasis in different classes. For example, using a science curriculum, one group of teachers may be encouraged or coached to encourage student initiated questions, while a second group is not. This emphasis at the instructional and experiential level of curriculum can be observed and assessed between groups to assure the difference between classes. Comparisons can then be made in student outcomes. The random assignment of individual students to differing treatments may be very difficult to accomplish in a small school population. In addition, personal factors of teachers may confound the evaluation.

Such evaluations of curriculum using different emphasis might better be done using the classroom as the unit of study and involving large populations of teachers from schools in districts or regions.

Analysis of differing curriculum treatments which can be introduced within the classroom have the best chance for random assignment. An example might be a comparison of the effects of the size of working groups at computers on productivity, achievement, and attitude of students in a curriculum for computer programming (see Case Study, Chapter 15). Such random assignment is under the instructor's control and not related to scheduling procedures for the entire grade level or school.

Quasi-experimental designs are used when random assignment to compared groups cannot be accomplished. In these situations an attempt is made to find a control group of similar situation and perhaps matched characteristics. A pre-assessment is done to determine the similarity of the groups at the start of the curriculum experience. Often an analysis of covariance is required to account for the initial differences between groups.

Most curriculum evaluation studies to be done within the school or even school district are a-experimental case studies. Such designs are appropriate to the context of a definite population and community. In this situation random sampling is attempted so that the study sample is truly representative of the population. Occasionally comparisons of curricula or methods must be made. In these efforts random selection is appropriate in an experimental design so that biases other than the curriculum treatments can be distributed to cancel themselves out in the assessment. Quasi-experimental designs make sense only when comparable groups are not available.

SUMMARY

Sampling is an every moment feature of our daily experience and meaning making. Careful sampling of events is important to minimize biases and distortions about our perception and understanding. Random sampling is one way to mathematically spread differences out so that a sample is characteristic of a whole population, or so that one sample given a certain treatment experience is not unusually different than another sample not given the treatment experience.

This chapter presented ways to select a random sample and a method to estimate how large a sample must be to be similar to its population with a high degree of confidence. The practical issues of sampling in the school setting were also discussed.

Most evaluation studies conducted within schools are of the case study design. One approach to the case study is to make a change effect evident by pretesting, posttesting, and interval-testing if possible. Most experimental-control designs are very difficult to develop in the school setting due to organization, scheduling, and ethical and political considerations. One practical approach to experimental-control studies of different curricular experiences is to conduct them within classroom organization which permits random assignment. Only certain types of treatment studies are possible in this setting. One very important use of experimental-control design is for evaluating a program which is viewed skeptically by school authorities.

Suggested Activities

1. Use a class list of students to select a random sample by two different means. Practice random assignment of class members to different groups using a deck of cards as a random generator.
2. Read the case studies (Chapters 13, 14, 15) to determine how sampling was done and what type of design was used in the study.
3. Interview a school district administrator to determine what policies and guidelines are used in conducting an evaluation study involving sampling.
4. Discuss with a school building administrator how an experimental study with random assignment of students could be conducted at a single grade level. What lead time, issues, and communication would be necessary?

Self Assessment

Having read this chapter, can you:

1. Select a random sample of 20 percent of students from a class list:
   a. Using a table of random numbers?
   b. Using a deck of playing cards?
2. Determine a sample size for a single school population whose average would have a 95 percent confidence level of falling less than .2 standard deviation from the population mean?
3. Describe the common errors in sampling which can distort a study?
4. Describe the nature and uses of different study designs for curriculum evaluation?

References

Campbell, D. and Stanley, J. *Experimental and Quasi-Experimental Designs for Research* Skokie, Illinois: Rand McNally, 1963.

Gottman, John and Clasen, Robert *Evaluation in Education: A Practitioner's Guide* Itasca, Illinois: F. E. Peacock Publishers, 1972.

Rosenthal, Robert and Jacobson, Lenore *Pygmalion in the Classroom* New York: Holt, Rinehart and Winston, 1968.

Chapter 10

COLLECTING INFORMATION
FOR CURRICULUM EVALUATION

As a result of this chapter, the reader should be able to:

1. List the criteria for making a choice of an information collecting technique to be used in curriculum evaluation.
2. Describe the appropriate steps for developing each of the information gathering instruments reviewed in this chapter.
3. Explain the advantages and disadvantages of each information gathering technique.
4. Explain the concepts validity and reliability, and some practical approaches to assuring the validity and reliability of information gathering instruments.

"Refinement of technique is no substitute for insight."

David Williams

The apple picker in the orchard is a collector of produce of the trees. The picker may take two tools along which amplify the power of one person to collect fruit, a taller-maker (a stepladder), and a temporary tummy (picking sack).

A paper-pencil test in mathematics is a tool which amplifies the teacher's power to collect also. It is an everywhere-at-once tool which puts the teacher in contact with each person, and it is a tool for gathering inferences (pencil marks) of a student's mental processes in reaction to mathematical concepts and operations.

There is little doubt that the apple picking gets what it's after, and is self-evidently a good or not-so-good collecting system. The mathematics test calls to mind the concerns we have when selecting or constructing any gathering tool. Does it collect evidence of the processes we seek? Did it gather evidence upon which we can rely? Does this method reveal what the student can do, can remember, can think? Is it an efficient use of teaching-learning time to gather this way? Should we have waited another day or two to set the test? Would we get the same thing if we gathered again?

These analogies of apple picking and mathematics testing are themselves image making tools for reviewing the criteria for choosing instruments and methods in curriculum evaluation. First, a collection technique should fit the needs of the situation and the persons involved. A paper-pencil test may be appropriate for many, for instance, while an interview may be appropriate for a few. Second, the collection technique or instrument must be valid and reliable. Third, the instrument should be efficient as well as effective to administer. And fourth, it should be focused. It should provide the information relevant to the question guiding the curriculum evaluation.

The following section will review some of the information collecting techniques available for curriculum evaluation. In each case the technique will be defined, and general steps for development and use will be described. Finally, some possible uses and the strengths and weaknesses of each technique will be summarized.

RECORD REVIEW

The school in its normal operation generates a comprehensive record of information about such things as grades and grading, attendance, behavior, tests of record, programs of study, course offerings, available and scheduled time, and purchased learning materials and supplies.

One way to use the records of a school as a resource for collecting information is called the data file technique (Gottman, 1972). A data file is a table of two axis to organize recorded information which is relevant to a specific curriculum evaluation question.

The steps to develop a data file are as follow:

1. State clearly and succinctly the curriculum evaluation question of concern.
2. Based upon the question, identify the units of study; i.e., low mathematics achievers and high achievers, afternoon reading classes, teachers with Masters degrees, etc. Identify and list this sample of persons or units on one axis of the table (row or column). (A large chart paper can be helpful.)
3. Generate a list of all the kinds of information which might be interesting to review from the school records regarding the evaluation question.

Reduce the list to the most likely to relate to the question. Put the information categories on the other axis of the table. Check to be sure the information category is found in the school record system.

4. Have the information collected onto the table from the school records.
5. Analyze and interpret the data file. Such factors of learners as school absence, early and late birthdays, age, sex, prior grade averages, and so on, may provide insight into the curriculum evaluation question at hand. The analysis of these data will usually require only simple "eyeball" comparison of ranks (correlation), or can be graphed to give a pictorial comparison.

The advantages of a record review using the data file technique are:

1. Much information already exists.
2. Computer information systems often make data immediately retrievable.
3. Staff members of the school can retrieve information and fill in a data file once it is outlined.
4. Record reviewing is unobtrusive. It does not intervene in ongoing learning, and the information is stable.

The disadvantages of record reviewing are:

1. The evaluation questions must fit the recorded information resources, or vice-versa.
2. Collecting information from records by hand may be very time consuming.
3. Storage systems for records may be disorganized, and some recorded information may be incomplete.

The main types of curriculum evaluation questions to which record reviews may be responsive are those which suggest that different students are reacting differently to an area of study, studies of grading, factors which are influencing achievement, and changes in learners over time (probably of a developmental basis).

OBSERVATION

Observation is defined here as the viewing of the school or classroom environment for the purpose of identifying (collecting) cues and impressions of behaviors and interactions, and artifacts by which we can make meaning. The focus of attention is usually upon the instructional and experiential curriculum levels.

Observation has been developed over the past decades as a very sophisticated technology in the fields of education and psychology. The volumes of *Mirrors for Behavior* by Simon and Boyer catalogue hundreds of systematic observation systems developed and validated for use in classroom observation. It seems that many investigators who are thoroughly trained to use a systematic observation system end up first revising the system to fit their own needs or situation, and then breaking out of the mold to invent and develop an observation system which captures a different aspect of the interaction process. The benefit of this phenomena is that there are many systematic observation instruments available, and that simple ones for specific curriculum evaluation purposes are easy to adapt or construct.

The basic process of observation must include being able to identify an event which is happening, recording or preserving our recognition of the event, and making meaning of our record of events. This process is sometimes very direct and sometimes very subtle. For instance, we may observe a student in our classroom raising a hand to be recognized during class discussion and question answer sessions. If we define class participation by hand raising, we can, with a series of pencil marks on the class seating chart, summarize who is participating and who is not. We can assume class participation is done by students who have studied and can demonstrate their knowledge. By observing hand raising in a less structured way, we may discover some students who raise their hands just that fraction of time behind the teacher's recognizing, and these students, though appearing eager and active to participate, almost never have to perform verbally. We may in this more subtle observation, have uncovered the well known and traditional "pretend-to-participate" game of less able or unprepared learners in the classroom.

The example of observing participation behaviors in the classroom suggests some of the difficulties of the technique. Observation is only a sampling of some events in the very dense and complex phenomena of curricular activities. What we choose to look at may be a very concrete representation of our idea (low inference) such as hand raising and classroom participation, or a very high inference relation such as verbal behaviors and thinking processes of a student. Other concerns about the observation process might be reliability, can others see what we see, and validity, the truth, for instance, that hand raising represents a seeking to participate in class discussion.

There are many forms which observation technique can take. Those described here will be unstructured observation, observation schedules, and systematic category systems, including category sign systems, time interval category systems, and time point category systems.

Unstructured Observation

Unstructured observations are those which identify situations and events *without a preconceived set of definitions or categories of events to look for.* Such observations are usually guided by a very general type of question or concern, such as "How is the new curriculum working?" or "What is motivating to these learners?" The record keeping system for this type of observation are anecdotal records or diaries. At some time after the observations and recordings, a reading and categorizing and synopsizing of the recorded descriptions is made which leads to a further observation and judgments about the truth and reliability of the analysis.

Perhaps the signal effort at unstructured observation for instructional theory building was the work of Smith and Geoffrey, *Complexities of an Urban Classroom.* In this study Smith was the external observer and Geoffrey the teacher and participant observer in the classroom. Each morning Smith observed and recorded events in the classroom. Each afternoon following school the two met, reviewed, and interpreted the notes. From this process, labeled by them as "microethnography," they were able over months of time to develop an explanation of how teaching and learning occurred in that classroom and some of the assumptions, values, and roles which gave structure to the process.

Unstructured observation has particular value in studying the implementation stages of a new curriculum, the way in which a teacher adapts a curriculum to his/her own style, problems with new programs, style and motivation of learners, serendipity, the nature of the teachable moment, and other subtle and interrelated notions of teaching and learning.

The advantages of unstructured observation are that:

1. It can be done anywhere, any time.
2. It does not set pre-conditions of categories, definitions, and rules about what to look for or what to call it when you see it.

3. It gives permission and ease for the phenomena in the situation to occur as it will.

The disadvantages of unstructured observation are that:

1. The observer may not be aware of or take ownership of hidden biases, cultural differences, or precepts which may guide or prejudice the recorded findings.
2. The reliability and validity of unstructured observation may be questioned.
3. The technique of observation and the interpretation of information is time consuming.
4. Observation (even unstructured) can change the environment of the situation being observed.

Observation Schedules

Observation schedules are the instruments which use general headings to call the observer's attention to certain ideas to consider in evaluation. A teacher observation schedule may include such categories as: knowledge of subject matter, organization, use of appropriate media, voice quality and communication, enthusiasm, etc.

This type of observation process includes written comment under the general topics based on the observation and interpretation of events which happened during a classroom visit. Such observation process does not account for how often or when specific behaviors occur. It relies more on overall judgments by the observer.

Structured Observation

Structured observation is based upon a system of operationally defined categories with an accompanying set of ground rules for making decisions about the definition of the category and the actual event occurring. A set of guidelines accompanies the structural observation system which explains the conditions of the setting and observation procedure which must be followed rather closely to guarantee an objective and content valid observation.

There are three types of structured observation approaches described in the literature: sign systems, time interval systems, and time point systems. The sign system does not deal with the time or sequence of events observed, but only a marking system to identify that the events were observed and how many times they occurred. Withall's observation system, one of the earliest developed for studying children's learning environments, was a sign system. The outcome of sign system observation may show a percent of certain behaviors observed or a ratio of one type of behavior to another (for instance facilitating behaviors vs. controlling behaviors). The time interval system is a structured category system which requires a judgment and recording by the observer at frequent, regular time intervals. The advantage of such a system is that the sequence of events and their use over time can be recorded, where the sign system cannot retrieve data in this way. The most widely known system of this type owing to its early development, rather uncomplicated steps and categories, and its widespread use in teacher inservice programs was the Flander's Interaction Process Analysis System. This system captured a rather traditional teacher classroom student group communication which was and perhaps is very common in classrooms, and used a three-second time interval which served to fit very well the communication and transition patterns of the classroom. The Flanders system was used in widespread inservice training, even with its limited category perspective, and considerable classroom research followed its dissemination. This very likely led to a proliferation of structured observation instruments which can be found in the Mirrors for Behavior volumes as well as other educational literature. Such structured observation systems were meant to be descriptive, but, for example, the Flanders system when used by supervisors was often employed evaluatively. This may have occurred because structured observation was one of the ways to quantify the interactions and sequences of the dynamic communication of the classroom, a phenomena which had been elusive for a very long time.

Time point systems of structured observation require the observer to watch a subject until a behavior category is observed, and then move on to the next subject, and so on in a regular sequence of the subjects. This method is often used to record and quantify at-task behavior of learners in the classroom. The case study of the computer curriculum in the following section of the text used a simple and practical observation system of at-task behavior.

The advantage of observation as a technique for gathering information is that information is gathered from the actual site of teaching and learning activity. It does not rely on what people's opinion are about what they do, or what they remember about what went on, or what they may believe would have been best in the situation. It provides quantitative data, for example, about student at-task behavior rather than what seemed to be the students attention or what a few of the best or worst students can be seen to do. A baseline of quantitative information can be used for introducing improvement or change.

One disadvantage of the observation technique is that it usually takes considerable observer time and effort to collect. This is sometimes a very impractical and expensive effort. Many observations are required to describe true and stable patterns in the classroom environment. Another problem is that the accuracy and reliability of the observer is dependent upon thorough knowledge, training, and practice with the observation system. The expertise of the observer with the content and developmental level of the learners also influences the data gathered. An additional problem is that an observer in the learning environment may very well change the environment observed and the behavior of the teacher and learners.

CONTENT ANALYSIS

Content analysis, in general, is an information gathering technique which is integral to observation. For this reason it is placed here following the discussion of observation. Content analysis is a form of observation of materials and communication. As discussed here, content analysis, as an information gathering tool, focuses specifically upon documents, instructional materials, artifacts, media, and textbooks.

Textbook adoption is a practical example where content analysis is used for gathering information. The checklist developed for review of textbooks is a primitive content analysis system by a district textbook review team. A list of characteristics is agreed upon which are desired in the text. Some weights of importance or value are given to the characteristics and some rating scale is developed. A review of nominated texts is made and a profile of their ratings is made. A decision usually is made following a thorough discussion of the pros and cons of the top rated texts.

A more quantifiable content analysis of a text is the readability assessment which can be done with a method like Fry's Readability Scale. In this technique, a number of lines of text are drawn at random from the book. A count of syllables of words in each line sampled is then analyzed, using a table which relates the count to grade level reading ranges.

Such estimate of readability was intended to identify texts which were appropriate in word complexity and difficulty for grade level learners on average. Such an approach can be criticized in the present emphasis on standards and excellence as aiming at the average or minimum functioning reader of a grade level, and in not accounting for the appropriate differences between subject matters in difficulty of texts. In any case the content analysis technique can be very helpful in assessing readability.

Any material or communication, written, spoken, or visual, can be content analyzed. The development of a content analysis system begins with a question of concern about the material. This question must suggest a set of categories which divide the question or problem into the variables to be considered. These categories then require definitions and units of study. These may be concrete examples of the words or phrases or themes which constitute communication within the categories. A set procedure for examining and sampling from the communication material is necessary and a set of decision rules must be developed which can be followed for determining when an exceptional communication is to be considered a part of the category and when it is to be omitted.

The computer is a useful tool in content analysis. Programs for the analysis of content are developed around categories and words or phrases. This is known as a dictionary. Written materials are entered into the computer and a search and statistical analysis is completed according to the program. This development in technology suggests increased possibilities for content analysis in curriculum evaluation of instructional materials and texts.

Another innovation in evaluation of curriculum texts and materials which seems very promising is the Annehurst Curriculum Classification System (Frymier, 1972). The content analysis of curriculum materials in this system is based upon the assumption that artifacts and curricular materials themselves have certain potentialities to *match* or enhance certain human characteristics which are involved in learning. As an example, a curriculum material which has many appropriate outcomes possible as a result of working with it, such as a piece of clay as opposed to a jigsaw puzzle (one correct outcome possible), is said to have a creativity potential characteristic. The jigsaw puzzle, on the other hand, has a self-correcting quality built in since the pieces will fit or not fit with each trial and the picture of the puzzle is fulfilled. This quality of immediate knowledge of results and completion is said to be a reinforcing and closure quality, and represents a motivational potential characteristic of the curricular material. The curricular classification system includes discipline, subject, and topic classification of material, age appropriateness, media nature of the material, the human potential characteristic categories of experiential, intellectual, motivational, emotion/personality, creativity, and sociability. In addition, there are categories for assessing the potential of a curricular material to be responsive to special learner needs such as visual, auditory, and motor coordination.

The procedure and ground rules for using the classification system requires training. The categories have been extensively reviewed for construct validity and the interobserver reliability for trained observers can be established at .80 and higher.

One advantage of content analysis is that it is usually an unobtrusive measure; it can be accomplished without intervention into the instructional routine. In regard to analysis of materials and texts, it can be accomplished at any time. This permits study of materials before they are purchased.

A disadvantage of the content analysis technique is that categories and indicators take a great deal of study and time to develop and validate. Further, a content analysis of many learning materials as in the case on mapping curriculum materials in use (see Chapter 14) is also very time consuming.

OPINIONNAIRE SURVEYS

Opinionnaires identify the type of instrument well suited to the survey method. Opinionnaires are used to help determine perceived needs or concerns, and attitudes, values, and beliefs of a large group of people. Survey method requires the careful preparation of the instrument, accurate sampling technique, and well executed administration of the survey procedure.

Opinionnaires are most often constructed to survey the opinions, attitudes, and values of teachers regarding instructional and curricular needs, parents regarding school issues and school support, and community surveys of opinions and attitudes regarding school issues, financial support, and educational philosophy.

Opinionnaires must be constructed to address the relevant issues and to communicate those issues clearly and directly. Given these objectives, each item or question of the opinionnaire should be written using these guidelines:

1. Write the question down exactly as you say it.
2. Write the question in as few words as you can.
3. Write a separate question for each issue you have in mind.
4. Say it simply. Remove and restate educational terms and vague terms which could have many different meanings (Any word with more than four syllables should be suspect).
5. Restate a solution or leading question which already implies how one should answer it.
6. Place a few easy to answer or engaging kinds of questions at the beginning as *warm-ups*. This will help establish the notion that answering the items is not difficult and can move along quickly.
7. A survey instrument is not the best tool to tap affective responses of respondents. If you have a few such items, place each carefully after a sufficient build-up of items and follow with change of topic or pace in the items so as not to preoccupy or *turn off* the respondent from the total survey.
8. Rewrite two or three survey items as inverse statements of the identical issues already addressed. Put these items in as checks of the respondents' consistency to the issues and the survey.

The advantage of the opinionnaire is the ability to get responses from many people with relatively little expense and use of time. The disadvantages are that surveys are much used and people may be jaded at the prospect of filling out yet another one. A follow-up effort is usually necessary to get enough responses to a survey. Another concern is that people may respond as they believe they should or according to their intellectual beliefs about issues rather than their true actions or opinions.

Rating Scales

Opinionnaires often employ a rating scale at the end of each item for the respondent to choose a number as an indicator about the item. The scale may have numbers 1 through 5 equidistant on a row at the end of the item. Each number may be given a word value such as 1 is poor; 2, fair; 3, average; 4, good; and 5, excellent. Some rating scales use only three place holder indicators such as: 1, rarely; 2, sometimes; 3, often. Many rating scales use seven step indicators and in some cases more.

Another much used approach to rating scales, often found in needs assessment opinionnaires, is the use of two rating scales for each item, one to indicate the perceived reality or actual practice, while the second rating scale is used to indicate ideal or hoped for states of practice. This double rating system is used to identify discrepancies or *needs* between what are perceived as actual conditions and ideal conditions.

Rating scales are also used on observation instruments to be used by expert observers in determining a quality of practice or action rather than a quantity of actions or behaviors.

An advantage of rating scales used in conjunction with survey opinionnaires and observation instruments is that they offer a precise way to respond to an item. Such ratings can be totaled and displayed by graph, or averaged for groups of respondents.

Disadvantages of rating scales are that they suggest quantifiable differences between, for example, a rating of good and excellent, where no unit quantity of difference can be made. The use of real and ideal rating scales on the same opinionnaire almost certainly ensure a built-in discrepancy of responses where none may actually exist. Another disadvantage is that ratings will be based upon different criteria from item to item and from respondent to respondent.

Ranking Scales

Ranking scales require respondents to prioritize items, for example, goals or needs, by comparing them with each other. This type of instrument usually contains a limited number of items, perhaps ten or twelve.

Ranking items is often done accompanied by a group process so that the rationale for placement of an item is subject to consensus of the persons involved.

Ranking items is an easy process to complete if there are a limited set of items. The disadvantage of ranking is that the criteria for placing items may change from one item to the next and from one person to another. Long sets of items make ranking distinctions suspect. It may be clear, for example, that the first items are very different from the last in the list, but the distinction between the seventh item and the eighth item may not be practical or valid. In addition, a ranking process forces some items to be last. Thus, it can be used inappropriately, for instance, in ranking all one's teachers.

Q Sort

Q Sort is a special technique for ranking items. It consists of items on separate cards which are to be sorted according to certain directions and criteria. Sometimes the directions call for a simple ranking or placing of cards in order from top to bottom of the stacks. In some cases, the cards are to be sorted into frequency categories which roughly parallel a normal distribution curve. The process allows a very helpful flexibility in the ranking process because cards may be sorted and resorted or moved individually. (A very simplified approach to ranking using Q sort can be found in the case study in Chapter 13.) The drawback to the Q sort method is that directions to respondents can be complex. The use of large numbers of items may also be a drawback because it becomes time consuming and the difference between single items may be lost.

INTERVIEWS

Interviewing is a technique involving all aspects of interpersonal communication including orientation, trust building, listening skills, verbal and nonverbal behaviors, perception checking, and paraphrasing to name a few. The personal encounter provides the advantage of checking and verifying what is said, restating questions which seem to be mis-interpreted. Probing for further information and managing communication about sensitive issues is also possible, but requires particular communication skill by the interviewer.

The interview is one of the *soft* data techniques which can be used in combination with other information gathering to fill out the meaning of information. Interviewing can get at interpretations and values and attitudes in a way that other survey techniques can not.

Interviewing is used by teachers with students in a diagnostic process. It can be used with parents, teachers, administrators, and community members. It is, in fact, the most used of all information gathering techniques.

The interview is generally conducted using a structured or unstructured schedule. The schedule is a set of points or items to be covered in the interview. A structured schedule is one developed along the same guide-lines as listed in developing the opinionnaire; be specific, direct, pose questions in simple language, etc. Sometimes a structured interview may include *look for* responses which can be rated as being a good or appropriate or more complete answer. (An example of this is suggested in the supervisor interview in Chapter 6, Is the Curriculum Really Implemented?.) The structured interview assures some stability in the information gathering technique when several different interviewers are at work. The unstructured interview permits a probing activity to follow up the main points. The interviewer is free to use much more discretion about how to conduct the interview. The respondent also is freer to provide whatever personal and detailed information is on his or her mind. Such lack of structure permits more validity as a consequence of not controlling or categorizing the items of response. On the other hand, the response to unstructured interviews is much harder to summarize or synopsize.

Telephone interviews are a special form of this information gathering technique. This form tends to be less costly than face-to-face interviews. The partial anonymity of the telephone and the directness of it as a medium may offer several advantages in expressing opinions. Telephone interviewing is also subject to the conditions of interviewing in a private home environment and is subject to the same reactions of people as the telephone sales operations.

Interviewing in general is expensive and time consuming. It is difficult to get skilled interviewers, and the information gathered is hard to summarize. The technique has great potential in getting at more sensitive issues, and also in exploring the reasons or interpretations which people may have about information gathered by other means. In this regard, interviewing is one of the techniques for meaning making which will be discussed again in Chapter 12.

PAPER-PENCIL TESTS AND SCALES

Paper-pencil tests and scales refer to those techniques for gathering information about achievement, aptitude, diagnostic instruments concerning motivation, interest, personality, learning style, and knowledge. These are probably the most commonly used information gathering tools about content achievement and learners.

There are generally two categories of tests of achievement which are criterion referenced instruments and normative referenced instruments. Criterion referenced tests are based upon specific objectives. Each item of such a test is a criterion for the measurement of a specific objective. The standard of performance on a criterion referenced test is a set of learning objectives, and the success of performance on such a test is referred to in some of the literature as "mastery" (Bloom, 1976). A norm referenced test means that the test has been administered to a very large sample of students of similar age or grade level, and the assessment shows a normal distribution over perhaps several thousands of test takers. This distribution can be categorized by stanines (standard deviation in nine uniform divisions high to low) or in percentiles. The assessment of further test takers is made against this sample population. The inherent difference in these two test forms is that items of a criterion referenced test which show a high percent of correct responses are highly valued as criterion items. Popham, in fact, suggests a method for validating school district constructed competency tests as selecting the items of a test trial which 70 percent of all students answer correctly. In norm referenced tests, items which most students can answer correctly are not mathematically useful for comparing students to a normative population. Items of normative tests which discriminate high scorers from low scorers are valued, while those which most students can answer correctly (can master) are discarded or not scored.

Teacher made tests are often the most specific indicators or criterion tests of the objectives which the teacher considers important (the instructional curriculum). Though it is seldom done, the beginning place for a school or district to develop criterion reference tests for student evaluation could well be the item analysis and banking of items from teacher made tests. Such *competency* or criterion referenced test compiling usually begins with selection of behavior statements of objectives or purchase of such tests from a commercial source.

The three domains of educational objectives, cognitive (Bloom, 1956), affective (Krathwohl, 1964), and psychomotor (Simpson, 1972) are useful conceptual schemes for critiquing paper pencil tests and test items to determine what level of response from the learner is being assessed. The cognitive domain categorizes intellectual units, forms, and processes from recognition and recall to higher order processes such as analyzing, planning, and judging. The lower categories of this scheme seem easily attended to with paper-pencil tests. The affective domain describes a conceptual scheme of categories to explain and organize objectives of the feeling and emotional response.

The category of attitudes and values are often assessed by means of paper-pencil scales or rating instruments. Most behaviors related to this category are better assessed by informal observation of learners in settings which call for independent choice making, social interaction, and responses of interest or appreciation. The psychomotor domain refers to behaviors of the perceptual senses and physical activity. The scheme of categories seems to be organized around a response and initiation continuum and a level of complexity and coordination of activity. This area lends itself best to performance testing involving observation often with rating schedules.

The advantage of paper-pencil tests and scales is that many persons and groups can be assessed with efficient use of time and money. There are many instruments available which have been checked for validity and reliability. Some of the disadvantages are that: tests locally developed are very expensive in time and personnel. Purchase of a commercially available test may not be appropriate for the local curriculum, and may force instruction to focus on the outcomes of the test as the actual curriculum in practice. A more generic disadvantage of the paper-pencil approach to information gathering is that it assesses responses of individuals which may not be consistent with the responses of behavior in actual situations.

PERFORMANCE TESTS

A Performance Test is an information gathering technique for assessing complex and holistic actions and behaviors in a real or near real situation. Clinical work and simulation are two situations in which performance testing is often done. This type of information gathering requires expert observers, and relies heavily on critical judgment or connoisseurship as Eisner has termed it.

The advantage of performance testing is that it can be used to assess authentic or real world actions. The assumption is that performance testing gives more assurance that behaviors assessed can be applied. The disadvantages of such an assessment method is that it is expensive in use of experts, in creating situations, and in the individualization of the test.

VALIDITY, RELIABILITY, AND OBJECTIVITY

Validity of a technique for gathering information is defined as the truth of the test. Does it measure what we intended to measure? Apple picking is valid on its face. It is content valid. The result of the gathering is apples, not stones or leaves. A content valid survey instrument to measure attitude toward school may be determined by the fact that the survey writers stated specifically and exactly what they meant to say about attitude toward school. The same survey could be checked for content validity by asking teachers of the school district (experts) to review the instrument and judge that the items do or do not get at what is wanted regarding attitudes. Likewise, a mathematics test can be reviewed to see that each item corresponds to an instructional objective and the behavior proposed by it.

In the same example of the survey of attitudes toward school, a predictive validity (the instrument is true because of a reasonable consequence) might be the belief that the school tax levee would pass based upon the attitude toward school's survey.

Construct validity, using the same survey example, would be the ability to understand certain logically sound categories or factors within the attitudes toward schools to better understand the true nature of that attitude. Such concepts operationalized through the survey items might be personal and educational philosophy, self concept, social valuing, activity press. Such a survey could be construct validated by experts judging or rationally deducing that the concepts were represented in the items. Other possible assessments of validity could be surveying groups which by some other means are known to differ on attitude toward school.

One particularly useful way to confirm the truth of an assessment is to choose a second method or technique. The proposition is that two different modes of information gathering which confirm each other is a type of content validation.

Reliability is the concept that what is assessed would be the same if it could be repeated. The apple picker would pick the same ripe apples again if we could go back and start the work day again. In the case of a mathematics test, reliability can be checked by comparing several similar items of the test; that is, if the student can do multiplication problems in one part of the test, he or she can do them in another part of the test.

A valuable reliability check in observation, interviewing, and performance testing is to use two data gatherers in the same setting.

Objectivity is the condition of gathering information which can minimize the bias. (The apple picker believes that yellow apples are always sour.) Several means to assure objectivity are: eliminate leading statements which imply what response would be *correct*, standardize how a technique or instrument is employed in data gathering, and specifically acknowledge what biases may be operating at the outset.

Objectivity is not necessarily a goal to be achieved wherever possible. The free rein of subjective impressions by professional experts may be a very reliable and valid means of gathering useful and subtle information.

SUMMARY

There are many options and combinations of techniques and methods available for collecting information in the curriculum evaluation process. Choosing a means to use in collecting information should be based upon the needs of the situation, the validity and reliability of the technique, the expense and ease of the method, and how well the question guiding the evaluation can be answered by a technique or method.

The information gathering techniques reviewed in this chapter are record review, observation, content analysis, opinionnaire surveys, rating scales, ranking scales, Q sort, interviews, paper-pencil tests, and performance tests.

Each method of gathering information has its strengths and disadvantages. These range from how expensive, interfering, and time consuming the method might be to how appropriate it might be in the situation and for the purposes of curriculum evaluation.

Validity was discussed as how true the information gathered is to what we wanted to gather. Reliability is the quality that information can be relied on. We gathered what was there. We or someone else would have seen it too. Objectivity is the notion that biases which tend to control information gathering should be minimized.

Suggested Activities

1. Examine the instruments used in a curriculum evaluation project and discuss the notions of validity, reliability, and objectivity.
2. Generate a list of guidelines and rules of thumb that you would use in determining how, when and why choose a method or technique for information gathering in curriculum evaluation.
3. Study all the literature you can find on a specific data gathering technique or method, and summarize your study in a paper.
4. Develop and validate a particular instrument for data gathering.
5. Review published instruments available for a particular data gather-

ing purpose. Critique them for validity, ease of use, simplicity of scoring, etc.

Self Assessment

1. Can you state criteria for selecting an information gathering instrument or method?
2. Can you describe the steps one would take to develop an instrument or technique for data gathering?
3. Can you give advantages and disadvantages for each of the methods or techniques discussed in this chapter?
4. What do the concepts validity, reliability, and objectivity mean? How would you try to improve the validity, reliability, and objectivity of a data gathering technique?

Bibliography

Amidon, Edmund J. and Flanders, Ned A. *The Role of the Teacher in the Classroom* Minneapolis, Minnesota: Association for Productive Teaching, 1967.

Bloom, Benj. S., ed. *Taxonomy of Educational Objectives: The Classification of Educational Goals: Handbook I: Cognitive Domain* New York: McKay, 1956.

Eisner, Elliott W. *The Educational Imagination: On the Design and Evaluation of School Programs* New York: McMillan, 1979.

Fry, Edward "A Readability Formula That Saves Time" *Journal of Reading* 11 April, 1968.

Frymier, Jack R. *The Annehurst Curriculum Classification System: A Practical Way to Individualize Instruction* West Lafayette, Indiana: Kappa Delta Pi, 1977.

Gottman, John and Clasen, Robert *Evaluation in Education: A Practitioner's Guide* Itasca, Illinois: F. E. Peacock Publishers, 1972.

Kerlinger, Fred N. *Foundations of Behavioral Research* (second edition) New York: Holt, Rinehart, and Winston, 1973.

Krathwohl, David R., ed. *Taxonomy of Educational Objectives: The Classification of Educational Goals: Handbook II: Affective Domain* New York: McKay, 1964.

Simon, Anita and Boyer, E. G., eds. *Mirrors for Behavior: An Anthology and Observation Instruments* Wyncote, Pennsylvania: Communication Materials Center, 1970.

Simpson, Elizabeth J. "The Classification of Educational Objectives in the Psychomotor Domain," *The Psychomotor Domain* Vol. 3. Washington, D.C.: Gynphon House, 1972.

Smith, Louis M. and Geoffrey, Wm. *Complexities of An Urban Classroom: An Analysis Toward A General Theory of Teaching* New York: Holt, Rinehart, and Winston, 1968.

Chapter 11

ORGANIZING AND ANALYZING INFORMATION

As a result of this chapter, the reader should be able to:

1. Display data in forms of contingency tables, histograms, and scattergrams.
2. Apply simple tools of analysis to changes in observable student behavior, relate one kind of student behavior (variable) with another, and interpret changes in pre to post-test scores.

"All the Indians in North America walk in single file. At least the one I saw did."

F. Owen

Large quantities of data are generated in a school concerning the curriculum, instruction, and learning. Grades are regularly assigned, test performances are recorded, perceptions of teaching and quality of the school experience are regularly collected from teachers, parents, and learners. Most data of these sort are stored in the information files (the archival data) of the school as a regular and natural outcome of the functioning of school.

Teachers, principals, and supervisors of all levels need to measure and make use of data for judgments and choices about the quality and effectiveness of curriculum, instruction, and learning. Such interpretations are needed to maintain good curricula and to improve the educational program of the school.

We could not possibly cover the useful and appropriate analysis and statistical treatments here which can be required in a thorough evaluation study. Several excellent texts from the reference section of the chapter should be good resources for addressing analysis thoroughly. We can, however, refer in this chapter to several very useful display graphs for organizing and interpreting information. We can also give a few examples of very simple classroom tools (statistical approaches) for getting a very general idea about whether learner behaviors (the experien-

141

tial curriculum level) are changing at the class and individual level. The limitations of these approaches will be noted in each discussion.

GRAPHIC DISPLAYS

A graph is an image representing a set of data in some geometric form, such as lines, bars, circles, bell-shaped distribution curves, and coordinate points. The visual display of information in this way helps us to see all the information represented at once, and to analyze and interpret it in an holistic way. Such a visual form is often a very good summary of a situation.

Graphic displays have two purposes: they are a visualizing tool for analyzing and interpreting whole groups and organizations of data. They aid the mind in creating a display. The second purpose of graphic displays is for the presentation and communication of information. In the first purpose we get the notion of communicating inward, where mental associations and discriminations are possible, where interpreting and meaning making occurs. In the second purpose we sense the notion of communicating outward to the various persons and groups who are to be kept informed.

KINDS OF GRAPHIC DISPLAYS

Bar graphs are a simple and easily constructed representation of data. This type of graph is excellent for representing different sources of a factor, representations of comparable behavior of different groups, and representations of change occurring over time. An example of a bar graph representing different sources of a factor might be the different sources of behavior of school children which results in school suspension over a year. An example of representations of comparable behavior of different groups might be achievement of boys and girls in some academic area. An example of change over time illustration by bar graph might be enrollment over a several year period.

There are certain general guidelines helpful for developing a bar graph. First, bar graphs can be constructed vertically or horizontally, but seem to represent progress over time better horizontally, and comparisons between groups or factors better vertically. Second, bar graphs should not change widths or be drawn with great width since this detracts from the representation by length of the bar. Third, bars used to contrast groups or factors should be shaded differently to make the contrast clearer.

Circle graphs are best used to represent factors which contribute to a whole in different proportions. They can easily be drawn and shaded in sections, and so are often called *pie* graphs. A few guidelines which might be helpful are that the contributing factors should be of the same characteristic such as sources of funds contributed to the school's budget. Environmental factors contributing to school motivation are much less likely to be comparable in character or in measureable proportions.

Line graphs are particularly useful for showing progress or the trend over time. Line graphs seem much more suited to a left to right orientation with the dimension of time or events along the horizontal axis. Two lines on the same graph facilitate comparisons of trends of different groups of learners during the same period or across the same events.

Frequency distribution graphs are known as histograms. These graphs are used to represent the frequency at every interval of the number of persons or scores. This display is sometimes drawn as a cluster of bars representing the range and the number of scores at each level. At other times a histogram is constructed by a single connecting line representing the number of scores at each frequency on the graph. These would seem on the surface to be bar graphs or line graphs, but they are not. The histogram is a display of area of distribution, horizontal times vertical dimensions instead of just length. The histogram displays a distribution by which we can tell whether the whole set of information is generally normal *bell-shaped* in form, or whether there are irregular, skewed, or modal characteristics to the entire set of information.

SCATTERGRAMS

A particularly useful graph for presenting curriculum information for analysis is the scattergram. This is a set of coordinate points representing two factors and generally showing how they relate. It is particularly useful in ·a needs assessment kind of evaluation where perceptions or real and ideal factors are being gathered on a standard rating scale such as the likert.

As an illustration of this use of the scattergram, a follow-up study was conducted of graduates of a training program. The survey identified fifty topics which the instructors of the program deemed to be the scope of the curriculum. The survey identified each item and followed it with two five-point rating scales. The first five-point rating scale was scored according to *effectiveness of training*, in other words, how effectively trained did each graduate believe he/she was on completing the program. The second scale (5 points) asked for a rating of the topic as to *relevance to job*, how valuable the topic was in their work. The outcome of the survey was a comparison perceived by the graduates of how effective and how relevant was their training to their jobs.

The following scattergram illustrates how this information could be displayed and interpreted:

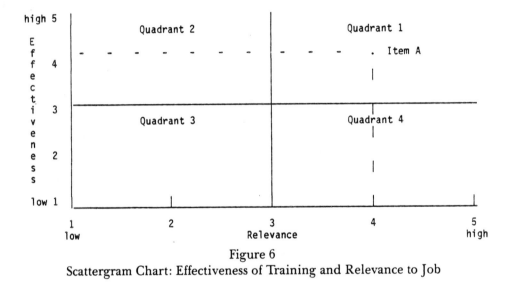

Figure 6

Scattergram Chart: Effectiveness of Training and Relevance to Job

Point *Item A* on the scattergram represents some topic of the program which received a 4 rating on Effectiveness and a 4 rating on Relevance to Job. We might assume that the instructors of the curriculum could take satisfaction that items in the area of the graph were perceived as well taught and relevant. Items plotted in Quadrant 4 would represent perceptions of topics which are relevant to work, but are perceived as not effectively taught. This could lead the instructors to consider two curriculum projects: (1) how to make these items more effective as a part of the curricular experience; and (2) how or whether inservice or follow-up training could be developed to extend the training curriculum for graduates.

Items plotted in Quadrant 3 would represent topics perceived to be less relevant and less effectively taught. This might lead to interpretations about whether these items should be dropped from the curriculum or studied anew in the workplace. Quadrant 2 locates items scored high in effectiveness of the program, but less relevant to the workplace. Items in this area might be studied further as well. It could be that these topics represent concepts or theoretical framework which is not manifested in overt activity of work. Or it is possible that the instructors would think of some of these items as important for future changes in the workplace which should be kept in the curriculum in spite of the constraints of the workplace as it is.

The scattergram can be used equally well for needs surveys of teachers or parents which compare perceived real aspects of the curriculum with ideal ratings of the curriculum as it might be. In such comparisons the real/ideal dimensions would create plotted points which could be interpreted within the four quadrants in ways analogous to the example above with program graduates.

SIMPLE TOOLS FOR
ANALYZING CLASSROOM INFORMATION

The following are three procedures for examining change in learner performance behavior, for relating one type of learner behavior (variable) to another, and for making some estimate of how important the change (gain) from pretest to posttest on a classroom assessment may be. None of these examples control for the influences of history (what else happened besides the class lesson) and maturation (what growth occurs in the learner anyway). The assumption is that learning occurs along with other things (history) and growing learners anyway. It is still useful to be able to examine changes happening in the learner experience curriculum level on a simple and timely basis. We can proceed to study from other resources and develop more sophisticated analysis as our evaluation planning requires.

COMPARING CHANGES IN THE
PERFORMANCE OF INDIVIDUALS

One of the propositions in the instructional effectiveness literature is that stating of clear instructional objectives as an advanced organizer of the events of instruction will enhance the program. The rationale for such a strategy is that it gives focus to all the subsequent activities and events of instruction. Resultant instruction and learning may be more effective.

It is an acceptable proposition at the experiential level of curriculum that having a purpose in mind for a learning activity can be facilitating and focusing for the learner.

To evaluate whether learners could state an objective for a learning activity in which they were engaged, a group of grade level teachers determined they would find out whether learners could state an objective for the activity with which they were engaged. A teacher from the group went to a fellow teacher's classes and moved about the room quietly asking individually each of the students what he/she was doing and why.

Twenty-five students were interviewed. The teacher wrote down what was said on three by five cards and reviewed all the cards. With high consistency (reliability), the two teachers agreed that only ten of the 25 students interviewed could state an objective for their activity. Each card which showed the student could state an objective was marked with a plus (+). Each card which did not was marked with a minus (−).

Following a review of the information given by the students, the teachers decided to employ tactics for a two-week period which would emphasize the objectives of learning activities. They brainstormed a list of possible ways to emphasize objectives during instruction, in the classroom materials, and when communicating with individual students. At the end of two weeks a sampling of student response to the two questions was collected again and judged by two of the teachers. Each card was again marked with a plus or minus. The conclusion was that 19 of the 25 students now could state an objective for their activity. Such data as these student performances were judged on a yes or no basis. The information generated is, in fact, nominal. It exists in two classifications of performance: plus (+), yes; or minus (−), no.

The McNemar test was employed to determine the significance of the change in ability to verbalize an objective for a learning activity. The following contingency table was used to plot the change in responses.

Each card had been tallied according to the signs:

A card with the signs +, − (could state and objective the first time, but not the second) is tallied in cell A.

A card with the signs +, + (could state an objective both times) is tallied in cell C.

Table 11
Comparison of Student Ability to State Objectives

		-----------Second Interview-----------	
		Cannot (-) State Objective	Can (+) State Objective
From Interview	(+) can state objective	A (+, -)	C (+, +)
	(-) cannot state objective	B (-, -)	D (-, +)

A card with the signs −, + (could state an objective the second interview only) is tallied in cell D.

A card with the signs −, − (couldn't first time and couldn't the second time) is tallied in cell B.

A chi square (x^2) is then computed according the following formula:

$$X^2 = \frac{(|A - D| 1 - 1)^2}{A + D}$$

where:

$$A = 1$$
$$D = 10$$

$|A - D|$ = the difference between A and D without regard to whether it is a positive or negative outcome

$$\frac{(|1 - 10| - 1)^2}{1 + 10} = \frac{(9 - 1)^2}{11} = \frac{64}{11} = 5.8$$

Having found a value of chi square to be 5.8, the table below can be used to show the probability that this change could be due to chance.

Probability levels and chi-square values with a value of 5.8, there is but one chance in 20 that this change in student performance is due to chance.

In this example of encouraging children to be able to verbalize purpose within their experiential curricular events, we can be sure that this improvement is not due to chance. The teachers might then wish to sort out questions for further study, such as, "What tactics can be helpful in improving unsuccessful students' performance?" "With what kinds of curricular events are children successful in verbalizing purpose?" "Does

Table 12
Confidence Levels Associated with Values of Chi-Square*

	(one chance in 10)	(one chance in 20)	(one chance in 100)
Probability level	.10	.05	.01
Value of x_2	2.71	3.84	6.64

*from Hough and Duncan, p. 348

verbalizing purpose in learning activities relate to achievement and retention?" "Why could some students not do this?"

This example serves to illustrate that any student performance which can be judged nominally (in this case classifiable as yes or no) can be compared over time intervals and analyzed in this manner. In many cases analysis can be done quickly and simply. What may be lost in sophistication of analysis is often compensated by the immediacy of the feedback.

LOOKING FOR A RELATIONSHIP OF VARIABLES ABOUT INDIVIDUALS

Returning to the preassessment of pupil performance, namely being able to state an objective for the learning activity in which they are engaged, we might wish to see if there is a relation between verbalizing a purpose for one's own learning and achievement. Such relationship can be checked by means of the Tetrachoric correlation. The correlation can be computed easily and simply using the table of values below (Table 13). Using this method and table, any two measures of the same individuals can be compared as long as one can determine those individuals which are in the top half of both measures and what percent they represent of the total group.

The following example illustrates this procedure using the example of the first assessment of ability to state an objective and the scores on a teacher made achievement test over the topic of that learning activity.

In this example our first step is to write: (1) each learners test score on a 3 × 5 card; and (2) a yes or no on the card (yes if he/she could verbalize a purpose for the learning activity). Step two is to arrange the 3 × 5 cards from high to low based on the test scores. The third step is to cut the deck of cards into two equal stacks (the thirteenth card in this case can be set aside).

We then count the number of cards in the high half of the cut which have a *yes* on them. This reveals that eight students were high achievers and could verbalize a purpose for their learning activity.

We then calculate that 8 of 25 (the total) is 32 percent of the learners.

Reading in the Table of Values of tetrachoric correlation (below), we see that the value of the correlation is .43, which is to say that there may be some relationship between achievement on the test and ability to state an objective during the learning activity, but not much. Inversely, in this specific case, you would not assume that learners who did well on the achievement test could have verbalized a purpose for their learning activity.

This study of the relationship of two sets of scores using the tetrachoric values would have been more appropriately used for two sets of well distributed numerical scores. It is very useful in considering any question about the relationship between any two observations or scores about a set of learners.

DID THE INSTRUCTIONAL CURRICULUM MAKE A DIFFERENCE?

When learners complete an achievement test, we teachers are apt to use the score and think about it as if it were something rather firm and definitive. As a matter of fact, one of the most useful ideas which we can use is the notion that tests, if they could be retaken anew, would result in different scores.

This range of accuracy of a score on a test is known as standard error. Given a single test score for a student we can imagine that if the student, completely innocent each time of the test, could retake it many times, his/her score would vary in a distribution of numbers, and that these many instances would produce a normal distribution with a mean and a standard deviation or spread. The chance that the one score which you actually got from his/her test paper could vary or be inaccurate by one standard deviation is almost a two out of three probability (very likely).

Diederich has provided a very useful approximate table for finding the standard error of test scores. Table 14 gives an estimate of the

Table 13
Values of Tetrachoric r_t for the Percentage of Students
Scoring Above the Median on Each of Two Measures

%	r	%	r	%	r	%	r	%	r
45	.95	37	.69	29	.25	21	-.25	13	-.60
44	.93	36	.65	28	.19	20	-.31	12	-.73
43	.91	35	.60	27	.13	19	-.37	11	-.77
42	.88	34	.55	26	.07	18	-.43	10	-.81
41	.85	33	.49	25	.00	17	-.49	9	-.85
40	.81	32	.43	24	-.07	16	-.55	8	-.88
39	.77	31	.37	23	-.13	15	-.60	7	-.91
38	.73	30	.31	22	-.19	14	-.65	6	-.93

standard error of a test by the number of items in the test with certain approximations included for those students who would score extremely high or extremely low on the test.

The following use of standard error for evaluation is developed from discussions by Duncan (1970.) When we pretest our class of students before a curriculum unit and again after the unit with a posttest, we usually have no control group with which to compare the change in scores. To make reasonable interpretations of the change as attributable to the instructional curriculum, we must be sure that the gain exceeds the standard error of each test. Only then can we even begin to talk about a change which may be due to the course itself.

To be reasonably confident that a gain from pretest to post-test is due to more than standard error, we must have gain scores which exceed the standard error of the difference of the two scores (Duncan). Let us take as an example 23 students who took a pretest on a seven-week course on computer education (see Chapter 15). Their pretest had 40 items on it which well represented the concepts and skills to be learned in the course. At the end of the seven-week period they took the same test of 40

Table 14
Estimated Standard Errors of Test Scores

Number of items	Standard error	Exceptions: Regardless of the length of test, the standard error is:
< 24	2	0 when the score is zero or perfect;
24–47	3	1 when 1 or 2 points from 0 or from 100%
48–89	4	2 when 3 to 7 points from 0 or from 100%
90–109	5	3 when 8 to 15 points from 0 or from 100%
110–129	6	
130–150	7	

items again. This repeat of the test was based on the assumption that a seven-week period was quite long enough for the effects of remembering specific items of the test to be minimized. Table 15 represents the students and their test scores. (This short-cut statistic was not the analysis used originally in the case study.)

For a 40-item test, the approximate standard error according to Diederich's table is three. If we wish to find out how much gain between pre and posttest would be needed to exceed the potential error of both tests, we would compute the standard error of the difference of the two scores in the following manner according to Hough and Duncan:

$$\sqrt{(\text{standard error of test 1})^2 + (\text{standard error of test 2})^2}$$

= standard error of the difference of the two scores

$$\sqrt{3^2 + 3^2} = \sqrt{18} = 4.24$$

If we round up to 5. we can say that the probability is 2 out of 3 that a gain of 5 or more points is a real gain and not due to standard error.

If we double the standard error of the difference (4.24 × 2) we can be 95 percent sure that any gain beyond 8.48 is real (not due to standard error). As we survey the table of scores (which might be arranged much

Table 15
Computer Education Test Scores—40 Items

Student	Pre-test	Post Test	Gain
1	9	27	18
2	4	25	21
3	9	26	17
4	6	24	18
5	8	31	23
6	18	35	17
7	7	23	16
8	17	36	19
9	30	38	8
10	7	27	20
11	12	33	21
12	16	31	15
13	12	33	21
14	11	34	23
15	8	27	19
16	13	34	21
17	15	30	15
18	13	34	21
19	9	25	16
20	7	33	26
21	9	26	17
22	5	9	4
23	5	23	18
Average	10.87	28.87	18.

like this in a grade book), we only have two students, numbers 9 and 22, who did not make a gain beyond possible error of the scores.

The average gain for the class is 18, which exceeds double the standard error of difference by 9 points. The probability is 19 out of 20 that this is a real gain in test score, and that we can begin to consider what contributed to the gain: the instruction provided, and the learner's other experiences (history) and the learner's own growth (maturation).

Using these three procedures, McNemar's test, tetrachoric correlation, and the standard error of the difference of scores, it is possible to measure changes in student performance, to seek relationship between two different variables from the same learners, and to determine whether gains in testing are real.

SUMMARY

The nature, purpose, and alternatives for using graphic displays are reviewed. Graphing information from a curriculum evaluation project helps the investigators to reflectively study and interpret the information and are useful as pictorial representations to communicate to others about the program. The scattergram in particular is a useful tool for interpreting needs assessment ratings about effectiveness and relevance of a curriculum or real versus ideal perceptions about the curriculum.

This chapter provides simple statistical procedures for comparing changes in student performance, for correlating one variable of student behavior with another, and for determining whether a change in achievement is greater than can be attributed to standard error of the scores. The limitations of these approaches are identified.

Suggested Activities

1. Conduct a survey of teachers in a grade level, department, or school in which they rate from 1 to 5 items which make up the curriculum design on a scale of actual practice and ideal practice. Average the ratings and plot them on a scattergram with the dimensions of actual and ideal. Share and discuss the scattergram with the teachers to see how they interpret the information.

2. Interview students individually to find out if they have an objective in mind when they are involved in a learning activity. Compare these responses with the teacher's judgment about each learner's ability to work purposefully. Using the procedure for tetrachoric correlation, determine the relation between teacher perception and student behavior.

3. Compare a pretest and posttest of achievement to see if the achievement gain could be due to standard error of the difference in the two assessments.

4. Take information which teachers in a grade level or department have available on achievement and standard scores of students and prepare different types of graphs. Share the graphs with the teachers to see whether different displays bring out different kinds of insights and interpretations.

5. Read Huff's, *How to Lie with Statistics*. Then examine graphs to do with

education in popular magazines or the newspaper to see if the presentation of information is suspect, using his five questions.

Self Assessment

1. Can you organize and apply statistical treatment to information about changes in student behavior, relation of two variables of student behavior, and the nature of achievement gain of students?
2. Can you construct graphs to interpret feedback information?
3. Can you use a scattergram to interpret needs assessment survey data or follow-up survey data?

References

Educational Testing Service *Short-cut Statistics for Teacher-made Tests* Princeton, New Jersey: Educational Testing Service, 1960.

Ferguson, George A. *Statistical Analysis in Psychology and Education* New York: McGraw-Hill, 1959.

Gottman, John and Clasen, Robert *Evaluation in Education* Itasca, Illinois: Peacock Publishers, 1972.

Hough, John B. and Duncan, James K. *Teaching: Description and Analysis* Menlo Park, California: Addison-Wesley Publishing Company, 1970. (See especially Chapter 11, "Analyzing Measurement Data.")

Huff, Darrell *How to Lie with Statistics* New York: Norton, 1954.

Johnson, Palmer, and Jackson, Robert *Introduction to Statistical Methods* New York: Prentice-Hall, 1953.

Siegel, Sidney *Nonparametric Statistics for the Behavioral Sciences* New York: McGraw-Hill, 1956.

Wilhelms, Fred T. *Evaluation as Feedback and Guide* Washington, D.C.: Association for Supervision and Curriculum Development, 1967. (See especially Appendix B by Paul B. Diederich, "Pinhead Statistics.")

Chapter 12

CURRICULUM EVALUATION AS MEANING MAKING

As a result of this chapter, the reader should be able to:

1. Give examples and explanations of the relation of meaning and change.
2. List the steps of an action planning procedure.
3. Give an outline for reporting results of an evaluation.
4. Discuss the type of school organization which would facilitate curriculum evaluation as meaning making.
5. Critique a view of the near future when career educators will be responsible for the quality of the learning environment and their own professional development in each school as a unit of change.

"Ways of knowing lead to ways of doing."

Madeline Hunter

The rational and logical conclusion to procedures of evaluation usually bring the final discussion to the reporting of information for decision making. For example, the definition of evaluation proposed by Stufflebeam (1971) is *the science of providing information for decision making*. The same work seems to conclude that providing information is the last step and there are many good handbooks on how to write final reports (Morris and Fitz-Gibbon, 1978, for instance). We shall certainly attend to good practices of reporting in this chapter, but before that we must point to and respond to the flying trapeze logic that moves from providing information to rational decision making. This is perhaps one of the reasons why evaluation studies are seldom done and often have little effect. In this chapter we intend to account for the nature of change and the making of meaning which fulfill a psychological more than a logical approach to curriculum evaluation.

155

THE NATURE OF CHANGE

About three hundred years ago in what is now Bulgaria, a soldier of the Czar would occasionally harass a citizen by pressing the cutting edge of his sword against the person's throat just hard enough so that the citizen could not speak. Then he would ask, "Are you loyal to the Czar?" The consequences of moving your head from side to side to answer *no* would effectively cut your throat. A short quick nod was the behavior required in this predicament. To this day in that area of the world, a short quick nod means, not yes, but "no." The moral of this story is that creating a behavior by force or manipulation will change meaning not at all. It may, in fact (as in this case) inspire a counter culture of language and behavior to preserve meanings in coded behavior which may long outlive the change agent and his law.

We see the world as we are and behave accordingly. Behavior which is authentic flows from the meanings we hold. Change which we undertake while we cling to meanings from another experience or time is painful, frustrating, stressful, and perhaps a presentation of self with inauthentic short quick nods of the head. Behavior which flows from new meaning does not require guarded self-monitoring, it is self-adjusting of false starts and mistakes in action because it has a constant intention, a compass of meaning. Such change is creative, generative of energy, tolerant of errors, and accommodating of modifications in plans and designs, because the orientation, the meaning, is known and valued. Changing one's mind is the essential condition for changing behavior.

Change has been classified by amounts (Stufflebeam 1971). Maintenance is a lack of change determined by monitoring a situation to keep operations working. The old adage pertains, *If it works, don't fix it.* Change in a self-improvement process is usually taken in small incremental steps, each accompanied by action planning and evaluation. Large changes occur during a complete revision of curriculum or program. It has been suggested that large change is potentially the most stressful and that self-improvement embodies change in more tolerable dimensions. The making of meaning is the compass of orientation for behavior and as such determines what behavior and what change is appropriate.

THE MAKING OF MEANING

The use of the compass as metaphor in the previous discussion is intended to subsume the nature of meaning. Likewise perspectives and frames-of-reference are now better spoken of as frames of orientation. The term orienteering in the scouting or exploring traditions means to position oneself in order to find one's way or direction by means of a compass or by natural features of the environment which can be interpreted like a compass. So in orienteering the last steps we took can be justified by our present orientation and the next steps we take and our will and purpose in taking them can be affirmed by the same frame of orientation. Meaning then is a frame of orientation which sums up the *justification* and the *purpose* of our past and present actions. The study of meaning, what it is, and how it is constructed, is the perennial human dilemma of philosophers, logicians, historians, theologians, and psychologists over many centuries. It is sufficient if limited to say that *meaning is that inner frame of orientation that justifies the outcomes of our action, while creating choice points and direction for our further activity.* As Dewey (1922) might have summarized, ends (purpose) and means (process) are bound together in action through our intention.

Meaning making can be an individual or a group process. The individual takes each action in teaching students to fulfill a frame of orientation about how learning occurs and as a result readies him/herself to choose and act to further fulfill intention through the frame of orientation. Teachers also work together in organized ways which create a cultural context and a collective platform or frame of orientation for the learning function of the school. We shall return later to a process of making meaning individually and collectively.

ORIENTING PERSPECTIVES FOR CURRICULUM

In Chapter 2 three perspectives of curriculum were described. These now will be discussed as frames of orientation, the structure of direction by which actions can be justified and purpose clarified. By orientations such as these each professional action may be justified and fulfilling of our intentions.

In the first frame of orientation (perspective) we discussed curriculum levels, especially the formal level of curriculum documents, the instructional viewpoint of curriculum, and the curriculum of the learner's experience. As an orienting framework the ultimate function of schooling is to facilitate the experiential curriculum of the learner. Our compass point directs us through the formal curriculum, through the instructional curriculum, and fundamentally to the learner experience curriculum. These three levels help us to understand and design the school program. Formal curriculum justifies and gives intention to the instructional level. It is a description of the plan of curriculum. The control theorist might look for congruence between the formal curriculum and the instructional level. The praxis theorist might look for the translation of the formal curriculum to the instructional level. The instructional level involves the strategies, tactics, methods, and resources to facilitate the learner experience events. Our frame of orientation must incorporate the three.

The second frame of orientation, the curriculum wheel, directs our attention to the interacting of curriculum design, instructional means, learning resources, and staff development as interdependent parts of the curriculum domain which are necessary for the experiential curriculum of the learner. In this orientation we must question the quality and effectiveness of each component and its influence on the others. Ultimately the frame of orientation holds the learner central again.

Finally the four phases of curriculum, inquiry, skills, readiness, and self development relate to the balance of meaning, behavior, and growth for the learner. These four aspects should be found in the curriculum design and in the instructional curriculum, but they are fundamentally states of development within the experiential curriculum of each learner.

INFORMING, DEBRIEFING, AND MEANING MAKING

The cycle of informing, debriefing, and meaning making begins with the people who implement the curriculum, the teachers. These people more than anyone else have the experience with the real situation to explain and interpret what the information means. They can relate daily and weekly events of instruction, textbooks, audiovisual scheduling, and classroom events which have influenced the data that no one else knows. Only they can validate the information.

Begin the informing and debriefing process by meeting with the teachers involved as a group. Items or questions, or observation schedule items are presented from the original instruments of the evaluation and the teachers are asked to guess what happened or what the probable responses to the items or questions were. This opening step of the cycle reacquaints the teachers with the curriculum evaluation study and rekindles their interest in the question and the kinds of methods and possible outcomes (hypotheses) for the study.

Following this expression of opinions about responses and outcomes of the study, the actual descriptive data can be presented. Graphic displays and tables will be useful to help show the composite and related nature of the information.

Interpretations of the data should be encouraged by the group. The facilitator of the group meeting can paraphrase comments and write them on a chalkboard. Teachers may describe what the information means, how it may have been influenced by factors known only to them. The interpretations, paraphrased and consolidated, become the basis of the formal meaning of the evaluation study. A discussion of the successes or high points of the findings should be encouraged as well as the areas of concern or need for action. It should be noted from experience with this cycle that teachers tend to be very critical and hard on themselves about their interpretations. They often need a positive and supportive group leader who can separate opinions from facts and who can keep an even approach to positive and negative interpretations.

A review of the frames of orientation of the curriculum is also helpful to place in relation the formal, instructional, and experiential curriculum to this study. The needs of the program in the curriculum wheel components should be discussed. The priority and emphasis of the four phases of curriculum should be reviewed as a part of the discussion.

Teachers should make a plan at this group meeting to lead further group sessions for informing and debriefing others. This inservice plan should probably follow the same cycle of informing and debriefing that they have just experienced. Plans should be made to inform and debrief learners, supervisors and administrators, parents, and board members as is appropriate to the curriculum study.

The meeting should close with plans in hand for further debriefing meetings. One last question which each teacher should ask him or herself after leaving the meeting is one of personal critique, "What has been helpful to me about this evaluation study?"

After a time lapse for personal reflection and for participating as leaders in further debriefing sessions, the teachers will have gained a readiness for action planning steps to improve the curriculum.

REPORTING THE EVALUATION STUDY

In curriculum evaluation as meaning making, the report should follow, not precede, the interpretation and debriefing of the prime implementors (teachers) of the curriculum. In keeping with the concept of feedback, the teachers should interpret and validate the information.

Reporting is a communication step to keep various groups informed and to provide a formal record of the evaluation study. It has been suggested by Morris and Fitz-Gibbon (1978) that the body of a formal evaluation report should be no more than ten pages in length; that an internal staff report should be about 3 pages; that a summary to inform should be but one page.

Morris and Fitz-Gibbon also provide a very detailed and practical outline for developing the written report. In brief their outline by sections is as follows:

Section I.   Summary
Section II.   Background Information Concerning the Program
Section III.   Description of the Evaluation Study
Section IV.   Result
Section V.   Discussion of Results
Section VI.   Cost and Benefits (optional)
Section VII.   Conclusion and Recommendations
                             pp 16–26

Their handbook makes many helpful recommendations about the specifics of each section of the report.

One additional guideline about formal reporting derives from the issues of evaluation. When releasing a report of an evaluation to the press, it seems very wise to write the report yourself, keeping its body to one page and releasing it on the condition that it be printed in its entirety. There is hardly a better (or worse) way to get a misinterpretation universally believed than to have it appear in the morning newspaper of every household in the school district. A careful attention to this mode of communication is in the best interests of school and community.

ORGANIZING THE SCHOOL FOR MEANING MAKING

A school where meaning making is the process for its actions and improvement is the culture in which meaning making extends to the curricular experience of its learners. To develop such a school is perhaps much like developing such a learner. There must be developed a climate of openness to experience, descriptive rather than judgmental exchanges between people, a two-way communication process, and choices made in a climate of trust which are intended for personal growth and corporate improvement. The following topics suggest some of the conditions which can be developed to support and be reinforced by curriculum evaluation processes.

Organization

The school which can function best in identifying questions and developing ways to evaluate its curriculum for school improvement is organized for two-way communication and decision making at every level of the implementation of the curriculum. Such an organization has shared leadership and consultation among its professional staff.

Many schools have a central council of teacher leaders convened and facilitated by the principal, referred to by such names as the principal's cabinet, Instructional Improvement Committee, or Program Improvement Council. Such a group provides regular communication and consideration of school-wide projects and goals as well as addressing program needs, problem solving and inservice plans.

Philosophy

A very powerful frame of orientation for providing a value context for actions and accomplishments is a "Living Philosophy". Such a philosophy is developed from a process of communication and trust building activities, problem solving experiences and a consensus making process which results in adopted principles by the school staff on such topics as:

1. How should students learn in our school?
2. What, therefore, should curriculum be like?
3. What should be the relationship of teacher and learner?
4. How should we be organized as a school?
5. Relation of Parent, School, Community.

The "We Agree Process" (Kinghorn) suggests a procedure for developing a consensus framework of values for pursuing the major goals of: (1) response to needs of learners, and (2) staff development.

Action Planning

Action planning is a key cycle in moving in a systematic way from an evaluation study to the intentions we have. Meaning is a frame of orientation which gives us the opportunity to make every action we take a step toward our goal and a fulfillment of our purpose. Action planning is a tool in which we set an attainable objective based on choices we have realized from our curriculum study. The objective is addressed by action steps. These action steps require resources, responsible persons, and a target date for accomplishment. Such action planning is a process of self improvement to address the new meanings developed from our curriculum evaluation.

Learners as Meaning Makers

As learners are involved in debriefing and interpreting the experiential level of curriculum, they may find school a place where it is important and useful to seek feedback and make meaning. They, too, can learn that school is less a place where they are to be passive and respond to the curriculum presented, and more a place where feedback is to be sought and meaning leads to new ways of knowing, doing, and growing.

The Professionalization of Education

One concept of professional means one who engages in a great deal of diagnosis in her/his work, one who makes decisions on which lay people, having no expert knowledge, must rely, one who engages in generating new knowledge as he/she works, and one whose licensed work group engages in governing themselves. The future appears now to hold promise of career ladders for professional teachers where master teachers will take increasing responsibility for inservice education, curriculum development, clinical supervision of instruction, curriculum evaluation, and school improvement processes. Curriculum evaluation provides a tool for that near future when educators and learners will use feedback to make meaning for growth and change.

SUMMARY

Curriculum evaluation as meaning making goes beyond the rational approach of providing information for decision making. It is the interpretation and personal meaning one gets from feedback which makes change growth producing and satisfying rather than anxiety producing and painful.

After information from a curriculum evaluation study is gathered and organized in display forms it should be validated or interpreted by the primary staff members (the teachers) who are responsible for program implementation and experienced in the reality of the situation. This group process is referred to as debriefing.

Meaning making is an illusive concept which can be defined as the frame of orientation (direction) which makes each behavior a person performs justified and which makes each future act purposeful. The three frames of orientation discussed were the levels of curriculum, the curriculum wheel, and the 4 phases of a curriculum design. Each of these orientations helps to justify and focus purpose of the schooling enterprise upon the learner's experience.

Schools would be especially effective in improving programs through curriculum evaluation if they were organized to enhance two-way communication, collaborative decision making, shared leadership, and where a living philosophy regarding school and an action planning process were developed and practiced.

The future holds the potential for more professional growth and status for teachers and a clearer focus on meaning making for teachers and learners.

Suggested Activities

1. Read the reference *How to Present an Evaluation Report.* Obtain an evaluation report from your school or school district and critique it according to this handbook.
2. Facilitate a debriefing group session with a group of teachers according to the description of steps in this chapter. You will need some data which has been generated about their program which they have not yet reviewed.
3. Describe the organization of a school for pursuing regular curriculum evaluation studies.

Self Assessment

Having read this chapter you should be able to:

1. Describe and relate meaning making to change processes.
2. Summarize the steps of an action planning process.
3. Outline the contents of an evaluation report.
4. Discuss school organization and the curriculum evaluation process.
5. Describe how educational professionalism might be enhanced by curriculum evaluation as meaning making.

References

Dewey, John *Human Nature and Conduct* New York: The Modern Library, 1922.

Kinghorn, Jon R. and Benham, Barbara *The We Agree Workshop* Dayton, Ohio: Institute for Development of Educational Activities, 1973.

Morris, Lynn L. and Fitz-Gibbon, C. *How to Present an Evaluation Report* Beverly Hills, California: Sage Publications, 1978.

Stern, Alfred *The Search for Meaning: Philosophical Vistas* Memphis: Memphis State University Press, 1971.

Part III

PRACTICES IN CURRICULUM EVALUATION

Chapter 13

THE CASE OF THE WEARY STAFF:
USING A RESPONSIVE MODEL AS A GUIDE

"Every productive evaluation is unique."

Bonnet

The following evaluation was conducted in the responsive model tradition. The administration and staff of Bell School had problems which they needed to solve. It was up to the evaluation team to help clarify problems, explore with them some alternatives, and encourage the implementation of a clarified decision-making process.

THE SETTING

Bell School is a private elementary-middle school without religious affiliation in a large metropolitan area. Its population of some four hundred students comes from middle and upper middle class background from all sections of the city. The school originated as a school for K-12, almost 40 years earlier as the design of an innovative school leader, since deceased. It has maintained a reputation for personalized learning and an academic, college preparatory curriculum. The pupil population is now coeducational with approximately 20 percent black, 2 percent of other racial origin, and 78 percent white. The IQ range of the student population is 79 to 140.

Bell School recently merged with two other private schools for financial reasons. The program of the three schools represented a K-12 program on three different campuses with the high school program moved to one campus only. The administrative leadership of the three schools at the time of the evaluation were wrestling with reorganization, and there was some indication that there were differences in the philosophies of the member schools.

Betty F., the principal of Bell School, had previously been an intermediate teacher and had served at the school for ten years. The school was organized by teams of teachers at the primary, intermediate, and middle school level. A principal's cabinet of the team leaders and school principal completed the school organization of faculty.

The teaching staff numbered twenty-four regular staff, with four part-time instructors and tutors. The average age of the teaching staff was 33 years. They were talented, generally innovative, and hard working.

The parents represented white collar or professional occupations. As is the chief difference between private and public schools, the tuition paying parents exerted a great deal of pressure on the faculty through their expectations. They were often in contact with teachers about the welfare and academic progress of their sons and daughters.

The attractive setting of Bell School was a seven acre wooded campus in a once prestigious older home section of the city. Two of its campus buildings were old high ceilinged houses of the previous era. The other buildings were constructed in school building design and architecture.

ESTABLISHING A RELATIONSHIP

Betty F., the principal, called an old acquaintance at the university on a day late in March to say there were problems at Bell School and to ask if an evaluation could be conducted for her. The problems, she said, were that everyone seemed so tired and had lost interest, and that perhaps they should give up on their demanding approach to personalized/ individualized learning. A time to meet at the school and to talk was set. Betty then said there was only a certain number of dollars which could be spent and that she would like to make out a check and send it immediately. This proposal was not agreed to on the phone pending the coming meeting. The check for the full amount arrived by mail to the evaluator the next day anyway. Such action was perhaps partly Betty's style, partly her budget need to get the money committed, and a suggestion of the urgency of the concern.

The meeting at Bell School was spent discussing school goals for the year, accomplishments and concerns, and the nature of the confederation of the three private schools. The concerns leading to the call for evaluation help were expressed again. The principal perceived great fatigue and a lack of spark by the staff. She believed there was a waning commitment among staff members about the individualized approach to learning, something which she very much supported. There was also a lack of clarity about what parents expected and how very much extra effort the teachers were committing to both the curricular and the cocurricular activities of the school.

After the meeting a visit to all buildings and classes of the school was conducted to talk informally with each and any persons available for a few minutes. Each was asked about accomplishments and concerns about the program and the school year. Classroom environment was noted including displays, interaction, friendly behavior, room organization, and active or passive learner behavior. After the tour, a faculty meeting was proposed and scheduled where the evaluation process might be discussed and developed.

After the visit, all the phrases and comments which could be remembered from visiting and talking with the teachers were written down. The comments and phrases of the teachers and principal were paraphrased into question form. The list formed was of eleven questions. The questions were purposely phrased to delete any particular words or manner of speaking which would likely identify a single staff member as its originator.

It seemed from the first phone call to the walking tour and visit with teachers that the situation, the symptom nature of the concerns about time, energy, commitment suggested a responsive model evaluation approach. This staff and principal needed a means to talk about their problems and have people in which they could have confidence to listen and help them clarify and seek alternatives.

REACHING A PSYCHOLOGICAL CONTRACT

The establishment of a relationship between the faculty and the evaluation team had to be developed further into an agreement by the two parties to commit their time and energy wholeheartedly, to trust each other, and to be open to each others influence. It was a significant step which had to be achieved or the evaluation process might accomplish very little.

The request for this kind of commitment was jeopardized by the fact that; (1) the teachers, already weary, would have to find additional time to devote to participating in the evaluation; and (2) the principal, by committing the school's money, had made the decision. If the teachers knew or sensed the principal's decision to proceed with the evaluation, it might become just another task for the staff, who were already very busy. In spite of the fact that for all practical purposes the decision to evaluate was made, it seemed important that the faculty at least be made aware that the decision point should be a part of the beginning of the evaluation process.

The agenda for the 45 minute faculty meeting was prepared to begin with a review of:

1. The need for the study.
2. The purpose of the study.
3. A review of the significant questions already raised in visiting the principal and staff.
4. How to do the study.
5. Who would be involved and how much time it might take.
6. A schedule of the events to occur.

DESIGNING THE EVALUATION

A part of the evaluation design was completed in preparation for the faculty meeting. The need to respond to faculty and administrative concerns about their program could be addressed by interviewing, listening, observing, and getting the staff to talk to each other about the symptoms, the problems, and the alternatives. "The Effective School Processes" instrument was chosen as a comprehensive interview centered protocol developed by the I/D/E/A affiliate of the Kettering Foundation. To precede such interview process, a clarifying of the problems and concerns was needed. A focusing survey instrument in two parts, School Practices and School Recommendations was chosen. The instruments presented a description of outcomes of an effective school. The response to the instruments requires a rating by an individual of what one perceives to be actually happening in the school. This is followed by the second instrument which asks for ratings of what would be an ideal state of the school on these same outcomes.

A parent survey would be constructed based upon principal and faculty inputs and approval.

The evaluation team was composed of a talented principal from a school outside the immediate district. This person had been a trainer in the use of the Effective School Processes instrument and was presently engaged in developing a personalized learning program at his own school. This person was skilled and a good listener. The third team member was a graduate student experienced in teaching in individualized learning programs and eager to gain experience in process consultation kinds of activities with schools.

The schedule of the evaluation activities had to be proposed for the faculty meeting as it would inform the faculty and principal of the time commitments needed from them, and the ways in which it would disrupt normal daily schedules of the school. Evaluation team members also needed to adjust their own responsibilities and identify dates to avoid in the suggested schedule. The school calendar also had to be considered for possible preplanned events around which the evaluation activity could be scheduled.

Overhead transparencies were prepared for the faculty meeting to keep the agenda focused and moving. The first topic was an introduction of the request for an evaluation and the symptoms which seemed to be evident that would make a review of the program worthwhile. Figure 7, The Need to Study Our Program, presents symptoms of faculty and principal which were observed on the initial visit.

```
        The Need to Study Our Program


    1.  Feeling of overwork

    2.  Dissatisfaction with some results or
        outcomes of the personalized program

    3.  High emotion

    4.  Effort which may be misdirected;
        lots of work with little result
```

Figure 7
The Need to Study Our Program

A discussion of a few minutes with the faculty was conducted with as professional a manner and language as possible so that faculty members would not feel defensive in responding to behaviors and symptoms seen by an outsider. The sharing and discussion confirmed that they were feeling and perceiving many of the symptoms and behaviors similarly.

With that step confirmed the purpose of an evaluation study was discussed. This was an attempt to make clear that the evaluation team could do nothing alone. Everyone was in this situation together. From this point on, there was an emphasis on the words *we* and *our program* throughout. Figure 8, The Purpose of the Study, outlines the discussion which was followed. The evaluation team with faculty help could take the leadership to get information about the issues and concerns. The evaluation team could help clarify and validate what the problems were. The faculty and the evaluation team could each suggest and examine alternatives available to the school. Beyond the examination of alternatives suggested by the dotted line, the principal and faculty would have to take leadership in making the decisions about future actions. The decisions would mean: (a) revising some actions of the principal and faculty; (b) challenging some actions, that is stopping something completely and doing something new; and/or (c) continuing some actions to maintain the things being done effectively.

```
┌─────────────────────────────────────────────────┐
│                                                  │
│           Purposes of the Study                  │
│                                                  │
│                                                  │
│  Evaluation Team - 1.  Get information           │
│                                                  │
│                   2.  Clarify the problem(s)     │
│                                                  │
│  -----------------3.  Examine our alternatives   │
│                                                  │
│  Faculty      -   4.  Make decision              │
│                       a.  Revise our actions     │
│                       b.  Change our actions     │
│                       c.  Continue our actions   │
│                                                  │
└─────────────────────────────────────────────────┘
```

Figure 8
The Purpose of the Study

This presentation was an attempt to make very clear the interdependence of the roles of the evaluation team and the faculty, to be specific about the functions and responsibilities of each, and to indicate when and where the leadership of the effort would probably shift from the evaluation team to the principal and faculty.

The next agenda item was to list and explain the Significant Questions, Figure 9, which had been gleaned from the school visit.

Questions	Teacher Vote for No More Than Three
1. To what extent and what parts of the individualized education should we continue to implement?	4
2. Can we organize ourselves to: Save time? Increase efficiency?	28
3. Are there things that we do which the students could do?	6
4. If so in number 3, why do we continue to do these things?	0
5. What options do we have?	5
6. Can we be as effective if we cut down on some things?	10
7. Is there a duplication of effort?	8
8. Does what I like to do infringe on what I have to do?	3
9. Do we have excessive parent conferences?	2
10. What are the parent expectations?	17
11. When do we say no?	10

Figure 9
Significant Questions

It was made clear that these questions were an interpretation and combining of many things people at the school had talked about. It was important to explain each one for clarity and to encourage faculty members to delete any which were not true, revise any which did not express real meaning to them, and to add to the list. Copies of the list were given to each person present, and they were encouraged to talk to each other in small groups about these questions and to ask for explanation and to offer additions at the end of a short discussion time.

The next step in the agenda was to describe how the study would be done, Figure 10, who would participate, Figure 11, and a tentative agenda, Figure 12. The first step of how to do the study was a decision about whether we should. Each person involved had to understand the effort and time it would take, the questions which could be addressed, and decide in the face of being very tired and pressed for time, whether class schedules could be disrupted for one full day and two half days to devote three to six hours of time from individual schedules to get answers to the questions.

```
Who Would Participate?


All Staff

Principal

Some children

20 percent of parents

Evaluation team (3 members)
```

Figure 10
Who Would Participate?

Doing or not doing the study was never in doubt. The motive in making the decision point clear was partly intended to reinforce the commitment of each person to engage in the evaluation process whether it was truly a yes/no kind of decision or not. Secondly, deciding on what to do after the evaluation was going to be an important role for them, and this seemed to be an example or an analogy of the faculty role which was to come.

The next agenda of the meeting completed the "how to" steps and described the schedule of events so that the faculty members could get a clear picture of how much time was needed and what the activities would

```
┌─────────────────────────────────────────────────┐
│                                                 │
│              How to do the Study                │
│                                                 │
│                                                 │
│         Decide if we want to                    │
│                                                 │
│         A priority of questions survey:         │
│              Practices vs. Recommendations      │
│                                                 │
│         Listening                               │
│                                                 │
│         Observing                               │
│                                                 │
│         Parent Opinions                         │
│                                                 │
└─────────────────────────────────────────────────┘
```

Figure 11
How to Do the Study

be. Following a decision whether to do the study would be a prioritizing of the significant questions. The third step would be individual reactions to two survey instruments. The first of these instruments would appear in their mailbox at the beginning of the following week. It would take approximately fifteen minutes to read and to rate each item with a checkmark. A few days later a second instrument would appear in their mailbox. It was to be completed just as the first. The evaluation team would then be engaged in interviewing and listening to faculty members, observing children, and devising a way to get parent opinions according to guidance and direction from the principal and faculty. There was concern expressed by staff members that seeking parent opinions should be carefully considered.

The schedule of events showed a Monday in which all teachers from each level would have to meet together to be interviewed without classes of children for 45 minutes. This would make necessary some very creative plans for the school day which might involve taking double classes at times, or films in the auditorium or volunteers, substitutes, visits to the library and so forth. The second day would be in class observations, and the feedback session two days later would involve conversations with each level team of teachers and principal and team leaders without kids again. Besides the change of schedule, each person was reminded that he or she could count on devoting three to six hours of time to the study.

```
┌─────────────────────────────────────────────────────────────────────┐
│                         Schedule of Events                          │
│                                                                     │
│   March 13            3:45 p.m.          Staff Meeting              │
│                                                                     │
│   April 2 (Mon)       8:00 a.m.          Set up                     │
│                       8:30               Observation                │
│                       11:30              Lunch                      │
│                       12:15 p.m.         Interview Intermediate     │
│                                            Teachers                 │
│                       1:00               Interview Middle School    │
│                                            Teachers                 │
│                       1:45               Break                      │
│                       2:00               Interview Primary Teachers │
│                       3:00               Break                      │
│                       3:30               Interview Principal and    │
│                                            Cabinet                  │
│                                                                     │
│   April 3 (Tues)      8:00 a.m.          Interview Principal        │
│                       9:30               Observation                │
│                       11:30              Lunch                      │
│                       12:15 p.m.         Same interview schedule as │
│                                            Monday or observation    │
│                                                                     │
│   April 6 (Fri)       12:00 p.m.         Feedback sessions          │
│                       3:30                                          │
└─────────────────────────────────────────────────────────────────────┘
```

Figure 12
Schedule of Events

Returning to the transparency of How to do the Study, the evaluator explained that, obviously, the principal and he had talked a lot about how to get at the problems the school was facing. In the daily conditions of very hard work with little time, this procedure would require at least an additional six hours of personal time, and creative planning for two days of unusual schedule for the school. They might rather take the six hours and rest than go through with this. At this point the faculty might have been thinking things like, ("We need to talk about these things.") ("...two days disrupted.") ("Getting away from the kids for awhile wouldn't be bad.") ("It seems pretty well organized.") ("Betty wants it.") ("...someone to listen to our concerns.") ("I don't like things changed.") ("I should be going home now.") The comments when they came were:

"It seems doable." "Let's give it a try." "It could help." So, with a few supportive comments, some verbal agreements and head nodding, the meeting was moved onto the critical questions.

Voting was conducted in a preliminary way by show of hands on which of the critical questions were most important. The outcome of the vote put first, "Can we be more efficient and save time?", second, question 10, "What are the parents' expectations?" The other high scoring questions were, "Can we be as effective and cut down on some things?" "When do we say no?", and "Is there duplication of effort?" In the forty-five minutes of the meeting, there was demonstrated a business-like approach and a clear plan of action which hopefully left the impression that the evaluation team was credible and that something worthwhile could result.

CLARIFYING THE PROBLEMS

All of the steps of establishing a relationship, reaching a psychological contract, clarifying the problems and designing an evaluation, occurred in an interrelated and fluid development. The establishment of a relationship began and continued waxing and waning throughout the study. It began with attention to formality and courtesy; it developed as familiarity and deepened as respect; it dealt with boundaries to the relationship and the willingness to be influenced; in the end it changed balance from one of dependence or interdependence of the parties to an independence of the client. Likewise, clarifying the problems confronted began on the phone with the principal, continued in the interview and school visit, and gained some focus during the faculty meeting.

The major problem prioritized by the staff had to do with time and efficiency. Experience with evaluation suggested that this concern with time may have been a symptom and not a true problem. Sometimes the feeling of wasting time can relate to: (1) different values about activities; (2) priorities which have not been set; or (3) too many competing goals or demands. Since a private school is by organizational structure so dependent upon the tuition-paying parents, the evaluation team began to believe that the second question of parent expectations would enlighten the first question about time.

CONSTRUCTING THE PARENT SURVEY

The question of parent expectations seemed to come down to expressions from the teachers like, "What do they want from us?", "We can't be expected to do everything." On the basis of sentiments like these, the purpose of the parent survey was to seek some priorities from parents about what was best about the school and its program, and on what the staff should concentrate its efforts.

The survey was made as a sorting of cards (modified Q sort) activity. Each of the nine subject courses offered by the school were listed on a single pink square of paper and paper-clipped as single stacks of nine cards each. A letter to parents asked them to take the paper clip off the stack and to sort them into their own order, with the top paper (face-up) being the most important, to the bottom, least important, according to the following statement: "This is the most valuable subject in my/our child's education this school year."

The letter also encouraged the parent(s) to make any comments in writing which might be helpful to the staff as they worked to improve the school program. The anonymous procedure was explained in the letter, and parents were told they could sign the letter if they wished, but that it was not necessary.

A second set of sorting cards (10 topics) was prepared on green paper. These ten items represented school practices in which the teachers and principal were especially interested. They included: individualized program for each student, parent conferences, teacher-advisor program, Saturday morning extracurricular events, enrichment studies, community resource people, tutoring, and others. The letter to parent(s) suggested that the school staff needed to concentrate their time and energy on some parts of the program. Parent(s) were, therefore, asked to sort and stack the green slips of paper according to how valuable the parent(s) believed the school activity or procedure to be for their child.

The choice of a sorting activity for parents had several purposes: (1) it was a doing activity which might stimulate talk about school between parents or parent and child; (2) it was more fun and different than paper-pencil surveys; this might increase response and attention; and (3) it could be done in as little as five minutes or as much time as interest permitted.

The letters were randomly assigned to 20 percent of the school population by grade level (10 percent for each survey), by means of class lists and a table of random numbers. The teachers handed out the envelopes at the end of the day to children as our random list indicated and children were told to bring them back the following morning.

The principal wondered, of course, why we didn't survey all parents on both topics. Neither evaluation team nor the school staff seemed to have the time or energy to process that much information, and the first objective was not parent involvement, but a valid indication of what parent priorities were for the school.

The teaching staff also performed the ranking of the school subjects in order of excellence and in the school functions in order of importance to the program. A comparison of these rankings with those of the parent sample would be made later to indicate where the staff and parents agreed and disagreed.

THE STAFF SURVEY

The staff survey was conducted for two purposes: (1) To get staff members to think about and compare how their school functioned, and their perception of ideal ways in which their school might function; and (2) to give the evaluation team clarity about where the discrepancies in staff perceptions were and thus to narrow the focus of the interviews and observations which would follow.

The survey instrument is published in two forms, the Inventory of School Practices, and the Inventory of Teacher Recommendations. The Inventory of School Practices asks teachers to rate descriptively how they believe their school functions.

The Recommendations survey asks teachers to recommend by rating the school functions which would improve the effectiveness of the school. Each instrument sets forth statements in the following five areas: (1) how decisions are made in the school; (2) how the school is organized; (3) how the curriculum is developed and taught; (4) how students accept responsibilities for learning; and (5) how the staff plans, evaluates, and improves the school's programs. The number of items within each survey form was thirty-five, and the reading and rating activity would take approximately fifteen to twenty minutes.

The forms were duplicated in different colors, and two forms of the survey were to be rated four or five days apart so that the *testing effect* would be minimized. However, both sets of the instrument were delivered to the principal at the same time, and the instructions about timing were miscommunicated. Thus, teachers received and rated each instrument and turned them into the mailbox at the same time. Such are the practical flaws of an evaluation plan in action. No one could be sure whether the ratings were more or less discrepant because the instruments had been rated at the same time, or whether the prospect of getting through two instruments had hurried their responses and made them regard it more superficially. Given the responses at hand, the ratings were summarized to clarify the discrepancies for the interviews to follow.

Each of the results of the teacher survey of perceived school practices and recommendations led to the identification of discrepancies. In the category of school commitment and decision making about their individualized learning program, it appears that: (1) the staff did not perceive themselves putting into practice their commitment; (2) they did not perceive that the central administration of the three schools valued or supported their efforts with the individualized program; and (3) they also did not perceive the teams of teachers making decisions about the program operation as they should.

In the category of school organization and structure, the staff had shown few discrepancies in their perceptions. There were, however, concerns about trust and shared responsibilities of the staff as they worked in teams.

In the category of Planning and Conducting the Learning Programs, the evaluation team noticed a break between the recommendations and the practices in using student information as a basis for providing learning activities. In other words, the evaluation team would pay close attention to the diagnostic phase of the program during our interviews.

In the category concerned with roles of students in their own learning programs, the evaluation team noted a definite reduction in staff value and practice concerning students ability to state purposes for their learning, to make decisions and choices about their learning activities, and students own awareness and responsibility for what they were accomplishing.

In the category of procedures and organization for improving the school's programs, discrepancies were noted in how the staff teams should function, and in the provision for teacher inservice and improvement activities, and procedures of the principal's cabinet.

On the basis of these findings, the evaluation team chose to interview the principal, the principal and cabinet (team leaders), and the teaching teams, with particular focus on: (1) commitment to the school program;

(2) certain aspects of diagnostic and prescriptive learning programs; (3) the student's role in this school; and (4) the effective working of the teams and the principal's cabinet in maintaining and improving the program.

CONDUCTING THE INTERVIEWS

The interviews and classroom observations were carried out according to the time schedule planned. The evaluation team used mainly an open-ended interview based on selected questions from the "Effective School Processes" instrument. This instrument provides a protocol of questions and follow-up questions in each of the five categories of the teacher survey. A "look-for" set of examples of appropriate responses are suggested, with a means to rate the actual responses heard. The interview is conducted by at least two evaluators. Following an interview, each evaluator alone rates the responses. These are then shared for reliability. Any discrepancy may be revised as the two interviewers share their perceptions, or they may go back to the persons being interviewed and follow up their questions again until they are satisfied.

During the interview sessions with each teaching level team the purpose was to provide a secure and receptive atmosphere in which the teachers could express their values, information and opinions, and could interact with one another. Each session was held in a lounge of the school, away from the children. Food and beverages were available in abundance. The evaluation team members took the lead with introductory comments about themselves, which included talking about their own work as educators and included some disclosure of personal concerns or professional foibles in an attempt to model a bit of disclosing and risk-taking. Following teacher and evaluation team member sharing in this manner, everyone was invited to sum up remembered points about each person. This procedure gave a bit of practice to everyone's listening skill, and emphasized that what each participant had to say was important and remembered. These "warm-up" activities were not followed in a rigid exercise form as in a game or simulation, but were pursued in a general and developmental way.

The evaluation team then began to pose the questions or statements for discussion, encouraging talk with each other and expression of agreeing and alternate points of view. Some issues became evident to both teachers and evaluation team members as the discussion developed.

Recently hired teachers had uninformed notions about what the individualized program was to do and how it worked. Teachers were often developing individual courses of instruction, and quite apart from these, were collectively developing the units of study curricula in teams. They seemed, indeed, to be expending much energy running two simultaneous programs, a class group education of textbook base, and a creative developmental unit approach with projects, activities, learning stations, and so on, which was a great lot of work for them, rather showy in classroom displays and activities, but perhaps a bit superficial. The scope and sequence of goals and objectives was not clearly guiding the program, and the planning time and procedures which were so necessary to the unit approach to curriculum planning were not working very well.

The evaluation team members were engaged in a *listen for* approach to the interview. They did not discuss the discrepancies which they heard, but encouraged the teachers to talk through how they did their planning, how they used their time, how they communicated with each other, and how they relied on each others strengths.

Each interview session was concluded with a review of positive points shared in the interview, concerns expressed, and goals or priorities which the teachers had mentioned.

Following each interview session, individual evaluation team members used a rating scale of the outcomes covered in the Effective School Processes interview guide to estimate the level of development described by the teachers. A comparison of ratings then was used as a discussion of what the evaluators had reliably heard and experienced in the interview.

CLASSROOM OBSERVATIONS

During classroom observation evaluators did occasionally draw four or five students together for a quiet conversation about themselves and their learning activities. Evaluators were particularly interested to find out how they would respond to such questions as, "Are there any particular skills that you are trying to develop or concepts which you are trying to understand?" "Do you (the student) have any goals in school?" "Does your teacher tell you what the purpose or objective is for your lesson or learning activity?" "Do you ever decide how you will do a lesson?" "Or would you rather have the teacher choose what activity you do?" These types of questions gave some sense of how the children were perceiving their learning experience and some idea of whether, from the student point of view, it was a purposeful kind of learning program. There was also noted much student project work and a great deal of student work on display. Teachers behaved in a friendly, good natured manner with serious work expectations. The teacher role seemed balanced among functions of information giving, diagnosing, tutoring and instructing in small groups, and facilitating behaviors for seat work and individual projects.

FEEDING BACK AND MAKING MEANING

Two days after completing the interviews and observations, the evaluation team had compiled the information, prepared a written report, and had planned strategies for debriefing sessions with the teaching teams, the principal's cabinet, and the principal.

The problem of feedback was not that the evaluators could not come to certain conclusions, but that the faculty and principal must reach their own conclusions, meanings upon which they could make decisions and improve their programs. Options seemed to be two. One, the evaluator could present the information and let the staff tell themselves their interpretation, or two, evaluators could interpret and ask teachers to check the perceptions. Because of the effort made at a trusting relationship and the half day of time that could be spent debriefing, the evaluators decided to present the evidence and share interpretations. It seemed to the evaluation team that the meaning making would be very important to further action planning. It was also consistent with the idea of how feedback works in influencing change. That is, if the teaching staff and principal developed new meanings, the accompanying change in perspective and personal attitudes would raise awareness of alternative behaviors and actions which were practical and worth the risk.

FINDINGS AND RECOMMENDATIONS
ABOUT SIGNIFICANT QUESTIONS

The questions which the teachers prioritized originally seemed in the end to have increased in interconnectedness. For instance, evidence about the lack of commitment to the individualized design of the program led teachers to create a superficial or appearance program and a self-contained program within each classroom, leading to great expenditures of time and duplicated efforts. The parents priorities suggested they were highly in favor of a program of basic skills which followed the individualized design. The teachers, on the other hand, viewed self and social awareness, and inquiry and problem solving as most important in the school program, and in two-thirds of the responses, did not rate the individualized program as in the top five items of importance. This dichotomy of parents views with teachers views may have been contributing to excessive parent initiated teacher conferences in a search to understand and communicate. This excessive parent initiated communication had led to a withdrawing of parent involvement programs by the teachers. The principal urged all teachers of an individual child to attend a parent conference en masse, partly because a private school must be client-centered, and perhaps because the teachers did not have a basic consensus which one teacher could represent very well. Such group teacher conferences were easier to schedule when all teachers were not in classes. The only time for that to occur was during team meetings and group teacher planning time. And so the cycles looped back through all the issues of program, commitment, communication, use of time, duplication, and parent expectation.

The recommendations which the evaluators could provide were intended to be only the external view of possible alternatives and solutions. According to the original agreement, the evaluators could not be effective beyond that step. The team recommended that before the next academic year the faculty and administrator: (1) join in an intensive inservice program to develop a consensus about their values for learning, teaching, and the curriculum in the school; (2) reinstate a home-school communication process to keep the initiative within the school itself to inform parents and to get feedback from them about their child and about the school program; (3) the staff organization for planning and working together could be efficient if the first recommendations could be dealt with; and (4) saying "no" and avoiding duplication of effort would require their best planning and communication skills as they addressed all the recommendations.

WITHDRAWING FROM THE EVALUATION ACTIVITY

The evaluator even in a responsive style does not have the same role as a process consultant. The responsive evaluator engages in a process of needs recognition, data gathering, clarification of issues, and the beginning stages of meaning making and the development of alternatives.

The process consultant role could more appropriately continue a relationship in further enhancing the steps of weighing alternatives and following decision points and implementation steps.

The evaluation team for Bell School had provided a forum for school staff dialogue, had gathered data to evaluate the issues, and provided some alternatives to consider. Adhering to good principles of feedback, the evaluators had stayed focused on expressed needs, remained descriptive, tried not to overload the staff, and made clear that the interpretation and choice about what to do was the domain of the school. Faculty members appeared less fatigued, more responsive in communication, and engaged in interpreting the data gathered. The evaluators offered to return once more at a mutually convenient time, if called upon, and identified one member to be in phone conversation with the principal in the future.

REFLECTIONS AND SECOND THOUGHTS

After the evaluation process has closed, there comes to each evaluator, and perhaps to everyone involved, the echoing effect of the experience. This is a personal remembering and critiquing of the experience, a feedback and meaning making process which can help one learn, improve, and grow professionally.

On the positive side, it seemed that the evaluators provided a great deal of time and service to the school. To their credit, they were good listeners, and stayed descriptive in feeding back what they heard and saw. The interconnected qualities of the evidence they found from several levels of the school suggested that the findings were valid. On the hypothetical side, it can never really be sorted out how much the problems perceived by the staff were endemic to a private school organization in which both staff and parents could choose whether the child enrolls at that school. The other issues which were left unclear were: (1) what did the reorganization of the three private schools have to do with these problems; and (2) the principal's influence in any school is so pervasive throughout every part of the school that it is entwined in any answers or meanings which can be sorted out.

On the process of this experience, it seemed there remained much to learn about just how to help a school staff affirm themselves in making new meanings so that they have the right range of confidence and commitment to take new steps. It would be very appealing, and perhaps self-serving, for the evaluator to find out later that the evaluation led to new meanings which were followed by decisions and improvement. Such outcomes are ideal. In the work-a-day world of Bell School, the self-affirmation and clarification of the issues led to some new understanding and improved communication process and renewed energy by the staff. These were the signs of success of the responsive evaluation process. From these dedicated people within the setting of their school, new actions would follow from new meaning, new energy, and up-graded skill to share and listen to one another.

Chapter 14

MAPPING THE CURRICULUM MATERIALS IN USE: INVOLVING STUDENTS AS RESEARCHERS

"... let every child be the planner, director, and assessor of his own education ... "

John Holt

This evaluation study addressed the general question, What kinds and quality of curriculum materials are used each day in our school? Some of the faculty and supervisory staff of Winslow School had become interested in, and had studied, the Annehurst Curriculum Classification System. They were interested in adopting it. The question developed out of a concern to know *What they were doing now* about curriculum materials and to establish a base line before they considered any change. The case itself is a bit difficult to report because there were actually two schools in the same district who conducted this study. The Winslow School, the second school to do the evaluation study, had the advantage of refined procedures and techniques from the first school so we are reporting that experience.

THE SETTING

Winslow School is a middle school of 707 students in grades 6, 7, and 8 within a school district of 7400 pupils attending seven elementary, two middle and two high schools. The district is a middle class, suburban community including two adjacent incorporated villages of adjusting racial composition with little or no industrial tax base.

Winslow School is known locally as a traditional school with a good teaching staff and more recently for its emphasis upon competency-based education, which is a district-wide priority.

This emphasis on the development of a competency-based curriculum led to an interest in better use of curriculum resources among supervisory staff and happened to coincide with the development going on with the Annehurst School in another part of the state.

The Annehurst Curriculum Classification System (1977) is a compre-

hensive design for school which is intended to develop a school environment for learning according to individual needs. Its schooling model
describes the interaction of the teacher, the learner, and curriculum
materials. Of the many aspects of this innovation, the two most germain
to this case are: (1) the system by which thousands of curriculum materials may be cataloged, filed, and made immediately retrievable by topic,
learner level, media form and other classifiers; (2) the characteristics of
pieces of curriculum material can be analyzed for qualities which have
the potential to relate to certain learner characteristics of an individual
student.

The major adult actors in leadership in this case were: the special
projects director of the district who had much to do with the competency
program, the curriculum work, inservice, and the particular interest in
the Annehurst System, the instructional specialist (supervisor), the
librarian-media center specialist, the assistant principal, and several
very active teachers of the Winslow Middle School. These people had
visited the Annehurst School and had engaged in workshops where they
became skilled at analyzing the characteristics of curriculum materials.

The long term goal for curriculum development held by the special
projects director of the district and others of that level was to combine
effective curriculum materials access and use with the teaching methods
employed in the competency based education design.

ESTABLISHING A RELATIONSHIP

Winslow Middle School had 44 faculty members. The assistant principal,
the instructional specialist, the librarian, and perhaps six teachers were
informed and enthused about the idea of using more effective materials
more easily in instruction but the awareness and interest in the project
by the other faculty members was yet to be developed.

A faculty meeting was given over to the agenda of the curriculum
materials classification system, the availability of inservice for any interested faculty member, and the possibility of assessing the kinds and
qualities of curriculum materials in use regularly in the school. Several
teachers who were informed influencers in the school were among the
previously trained group and were responsible for a part of the meeting
presentation.

We had learned from the previous study in another school in the
district that students could monitor and record their own use of curricu-

lum materials during a complete school day and we proposed to develop that type of design for the Winslow School Study to minimize the amount of extra effort the study would require of these hard-working teachers.

The issue of good curriculum materials was discussed in a variety of ways and personal experiences were recounted of visits to the Annehurst School in Westerville, Ohio where the classification system was developed. Offers were made to support visits by other faculty members to the Annehurst School by the Project Director.

REACHING A PSYCHOLOGICAL CONTRACT

There comes a time in a working relationship between people when alternate monologues diminish and dialogue flourishes, where people find a joint project to make sense, to be meaningful, and to have some future relevance and benefit. We were hoping to develop that psychological agreement with all the faculty to proceed with the study.

Several faculty members expressed support. We had presented a relevant issue about good curriculum materials, relied upon informal teacher leaders in the school, and presented a plan for students to record their own use of materials.

Teachers did not appear overly concerned about the recording of curriculum materials. No one was going to observe their teaching. Only occasionally would a person enter a classroom to see if the children were keeping their logs accurately. We discussed whether this would distract kids from their work. The opinion of teachers from the other district school to pursue this study was that it did not distract from learning activities. The faculty wanted to know which kids and perhaps it should be only the most able.

The project director was committed to use ten percent of the students in each grade level by random selection. Only in a rare case like a disability would he consider replacing a child selected. The primary actors in conducting the study could sense a more passive acceptance of the idea among the faculty. They, after all, were not to be observed, did not have to do the recording, and were being encouraged by fellow colleagues. The use of students to record curriculum materials used was a paradoxical benefit. It made the study more efficient but put the teachers in a responsive instead of an active mode.

Teachers also wanted to know what they should do in their classes and lessons and were assured that exactly what they had planned to do anyway was what was necessary. Teachers were asked to give one extra copy of a ditto or teacher produced curriculum material to the student in their class carrying a recording log on the days of the study. If certain materials, tests and other special exercises were not to be shared or were being restricted for use in other classes as well, a teacher was to inform or share that item with the leadership group for a few minutes at the end of the day.

An agreement about conducting the study was concluded more by head nodding and other gestures than an actual vote. The principal, not much involved in the proceedings up to this point, spelled out the schedule of the study with a rather low key appeal to authority about doing the study which was helpful in maintaining the nature of a considered decision.

DESIGNING THE EVALUATION

Specific questions were addressed which focused on the following:

1. The time interval a curriculum material was used;
2. The number of materials a learner used during a day;
3. The group mode in which the learner worked;
4. The media form of the material;
5. The topic, subject, and discipline area of the material;
6. The quality characteristics of the material for motivation, intelligence, creativity, etc.; and
7. The age level appropriateness of the material.

The plan of the study was modified from the Shadow Study of learners done by Davis and Frymier (1977). Fifteen percent of all students by grade level were randomly selected using class lists. Study hall times of each selected student's schedule were added to the roster so that each student could be called to attend a fifteen-minute training session. At these sessions, the idea of the curriculum materials study was explained and they were asked if they would be one of the researchers for the following school day. Those who chose to do so (all) were then presented with a log of several pages (see Figure 13) stapled to a 10 × 12 inch sheet of cardboard. With this log, the students used the first sheet to practice recording a brief simulated set of learning activities presented by the project director. After a few minutes, the practice log was checked to see if the students understood the procedure and could record times accurately. The student was asked to begin with the first event of the following day, the Pledge of Allegiance, and continue through each class during the day. The student was to identify page numbers and textbooks on the log and was to collect a copy of each handout or other curriculum material used. A film or model was to be identified by name on the log. At the end of the following day, each student was to come to the library two minutes before the closing bell to deliver his/her log and collected materials to the librarian. Teachers were informed on attendance reports which students were keeping a log during the day and were encouraged to dismiss these just before the closing bell.

| Start Time | Stop Time | Setting | | | Name of Curriculum Material Used | Pages | Notes |
		Whole Group	Small Group	Ind. Study			

Figure 13
Student Recording Chart of Curriculum Materials Used

The logs and materials would be analyzed during evening hours by volunteers from the teacher group trained in the classification system.

STUDENTS AS RESEARCHERS

We who selected and prepared the students to log the events and materials of their school day while they were functioning also as learners, were none too confident they could remember their logs on the following morning or keep in touch with the log throughout the day.

The students, on the other hand, took this selection as a kind of special recognition and responsibility. They performed their recording task dutifully and accurately. By random selection again, an adult went to a room each period of each day to observe for ten minutes and to record what curriculum materials the student observer was using. The accuracy was .93 when the adult observers record was compared with each log during the observation time. Students also began to add comments and remarks at the side of their log about the quality or value of the material. We believe that contrary to the notion of distracting these students, it actually may have heightened their awareness of their learning experience, what they were doing, its purpose, and what things were interesting or useful.

ANALYSIS OF CURRICULUM MATERIALS

Curriculum materials, texts, and media materials were collected in the library each evening according to the student logs. These curriculum materials were classified by a volunteer group of teachers who have been trained in the classification system. Each item was classified by topic, subject, and discipline, group mode of instruction, time duration of the learning event, media form of the material, age range appropriateness, and characteristics of the material as high or low in experience potential, intelligence, motivation, ego-personality, creativity, and social potential.

In the ten day period of the observations, 91 learners logged 1,339 curriculum materials which were cataloged and analyzed. The range of items dealt with by an individual learner in one school day was 7 to 42. The average number of items was 13. The large modal distribution of items by single learners at or near 13 would lead one to wonder if the learning program is quite uniform for all learners of a grade level. Most curriculum events occurred as large group activities. Only 12 percent of the events occurred in small groups. Almost one-third of the curriculum materials were worksheets, while concrete objects, models, equipment, and actual things made up about 12 percent of the curriculum materials.

Curriculum materials in language arts, history, and mathematics made up 60 percent of all the materials. Most materials (91.2) percent were judged not to demand a "high intelligence response." Forty percent of materials were classified as high in motivational potential. There were also very few materials (12 percent) which had potential to evoke a creative learner response.

The information was summarized in numbers and percentages according to the specific questions posed, and were made up on overhead transparencies to share with the faculty.

FEEDING BACK AND MAKING MEANING

The teachers of Winslow school were able to explain such things as unusually high percentages and kinds of curriculum materials identified on different days owing to the type of special topics or media which they had planned and used. We got the impression that these profiles of curriculum materials might fluctuate daily and weekly according to teacher plans.

Teachers were concerned with what ought to be the case regarding the data organized and presented. They had a tendency to be critical of themselves and their programs when information was unusually high or low. Teachers began to discuss implications of the study for selecting quality materials and for making more materials more easily available.

WITHDRAWING FROM THE ACTIVITY

The study itself was an attempt to establish a descriptive baseline of the character and use of curriculum materials in Winslow School. The evaluation closed with a heightened awareness of curriculum materials use. The initiative for further action resided with the district project director. Further events by his initiative followed. A teacher newsletter was begun to announce curriculum materials acquired and to describe and give recognition to individual teachers who had constructed or composed and shared a teacher made curriculum material. All duplicatable materials in a subject area by grade level which could be classified by the competency education objectives were copied and organized in a set of file or storage cabinets in each school of the district. These files were placed with access to the school duplicating machine. The project director developed a computer program for the identification and access of curriculum materials in each building and across the school district. These events were not the initiative of the Winslow School, but awareness of faculty of the school about curriculum materials and quality of them had been heightened. Teachers became a bit more discriminating about materials used, and seemed to shift their notion from curriculum materials as something to teach to curriculum materials as a resource. It also seemed that the more materials to become stored and available, the more different approaches were considered.

REFLECTIONS AND SECOND THOUGHTS

It seems that the curriculum materials study carried out in the first school (not reported here) had much more participation and staff enthusiasm than the study at Winslow School. This may be due to size; the first school had 24 teachers, Winslow had 44. Or orientation of staff may contribute; the first school was an elementary school, while Winslow was a middle school. It is also possible that the study at Winslow was too smooth and did not require enough of the staff or have enough vulnerability of trial and error to elicit the involvement and empathy of the staff. It may also be the case that the purpose of the evaluation study (as in Chapter 1) may have been more so for intervention than for meaning making. The activities which followed were very much focused on improving the materials availability and the competency education program.

A second reflection about the study is that *learners have great potential to investigate and reflect on their own learning experiences.* The events log may actually heighten their awareness of their learning experiences. This might be used strategically to help certain students with management of their learning. It also suggests the possibility of an entirely different form of assessment and debriefing of learners concerning their own experiences and achievement.

References

1. Davis, O. L. and Frymier, J. R. An Investigation of Learners' Use of Curriculum Materials paper presented at the American Educational Research Association Annual Conference, 1977.
2. Frymier, Jack R. *Annehurst Curriculum Classification System* West LaFayette, Indiana: Kappa Delta Pi, 1977.

Chapter 15

THE COMPUTER CURRICULUM EVALUATION USING AN EXPERIMENTAL DESIGN

RAYMOND R. SPAULDING, ED.D.

Computer facilities and curriculum are an expensive investment for any school or school district. There seem to be two approaches to the purchase and installation of computers. One is to identify a double classroom sized space as a laboratory and install perhaps 30 terminals and appropriate furniture very much in the way the typing room might be set up in high school. A second approach is to purchase a few units and install one terminal in each second or third room throughout the building. This study arose because of a third design option of facilities and curriculum for computers.

Warren Hornsby (1983) developed and installed in a regular-sized classroom an arrangement of ten computers and one teacher (master) consul such that three students could be positioned in front of each computer (one person at the keyboard and one seated just beside each shoulder and slightly behind the keyboard operator). This team type arrangement with the keyboard operator rotating among the three in some regular way, he called the *pod* concept.

The system had many apparent advantages. The obvious savings of investment in computer hardware and the use of any regular-sized classroom space for the lab were attractive benefits to planners and administrators. Students with little experience would not feel intimidated and could benefit from the team approach (three people versus one computer). Given five periods of the school day and six or seven weeks course length, all children in a school of 600 or more could be introduced to computers in a single academic year. By the time Armour Junior High School administrators considered the investment and installation of computers at their school, the pod concept was being used in ten schools in the same geographic region. There was an obvious dollar savings to the design but no one knew what effect this design had upon the learners. Did they learn well in groups? Were they missing something without constant keyboard contact with the computer? What attitudes developed as a consequence of this approach?

Armour Junior High is a school of 750 students of grades 6, 7, and 8. The students served by Armour are of lower middle class background and are considered to be quite near the national averages and ranges on normal standardized tests. Its staff could be described as both experienced and dedicated with good rapport with students. Students and staff alike take an unusual sense of pride in the cleanliness and appearance of the school property. The curriculum and instructional program of the school could be described as traditional.

THE POD CONCEPT

The pod concept is a special system of grouping students around the computers in order to reach the goal of effectively teaching the maximum number of students with the minimum amount of computer hardware. While only one student at a time actually operates the computer, the remaining students in the pod have a direct line of sight to the computer screen and are a vital part of the learning team. Students are then rotated usually on a daily basis to give *hands on* experience for each member of the pod.

The benefits of the pod concept as observed in several nearby schools were:

1. Students working together in a pod were able to solve many of the operating procedures that might be confusing for only one student.
2. Students learned from each other. Brainstorming became the norm when programming and debugging got underway.
3. The atmosphere at the computer was reassuring to new computer students. It's three students vs. one computer.

THE QUALITY OF LEARNING EXPERIENCE

No one knew whether student learning was in some way being sacrificed by this small group method in the computer program. A financial savings on one hand might lead to a lack of achievement by students and,

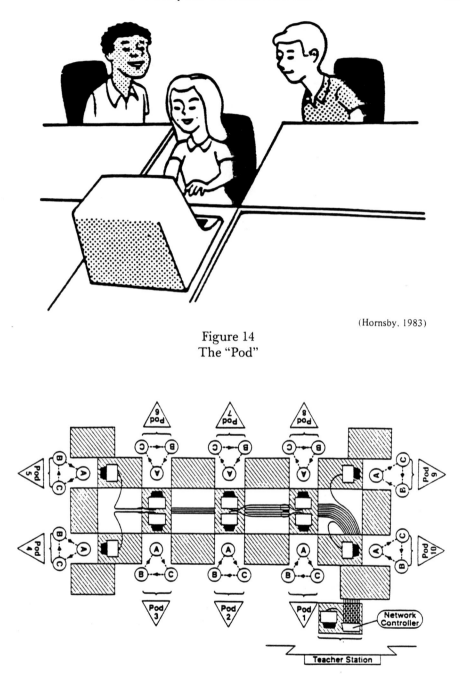

(Hornsby, 1983)

Figure 14
The "Pod"

(Hornsby, 1983)

Figure 15
The "Pod" Concept

perhaps even more critical, a negative reaction to the program by students and then parents.

A thorough discussion of the factors about a student's learning experience led to the identification of four important considerations. First, students should be able to achieve the course content equally. Second, students working in groups (pods) should show equivalent *at task* behavior as those working alone. Third, students should display similar positive attitudes whether working in groups or singly. And, fourth, students working in groups should be as productive (get as much work done) as those working alone. If these characteristics of their work were similar perhaps the pod concept was a satisfactory computer curriculum design.

PROCEDURE

Students were assigned to classes of the 10 unit computer laboratory employing the student group (pod) plan by the school principal using standard school scheduling procedures. Two seventh and two eighth grade classes were chosen for the evaluation study which could be schedule with less than 30 students. Within these four classes, using class lists, students were randomly assigned to computer singly, or in pairs, or in the trio suggested by the pod design. The total arrangements in all four classes was 16 groups of three students (pods), 18 pairs of students and 7 single student assignments to computers.

The combinations constituted 41 groups in 4 classes with 40 computer terminals available. The extra station was accomplished by adding an extra microcomputer. The four classes totaled 87 students instead of the capacity of the design for that many classes (120 students). This reduced class membership made the experimental design possible.

Curriculum for the class instruction used the Life Skills Program by SVE Singer Corporation entitled, Introduction to Computers (Life Skills, 1981). To ensure equal time and consistent emphasis of instructional content in all four classes, course lesson plans were prepared and followed. The evaluator worked closely with the computer classroom teacher on a daily basis to monitor and assist in the day-to-day activities which occurred. The support of the school administration was also secured to assist with scheduling problems, and to assist in keeping the class size at a workable level for the evaluation.

INSTRUMENTS

Four measurement instruments were used in the evaluation. A forty-item test was developed from the lesson quizzes of the SVE Singer Program. This achievement test was used as a pretest on the first day of the course and as a posttest to measure change in achievement (see Chapter 11, Organizing and Analyzing Information). An attitude instrument was developed to determine student opinions about computers, attitude toward the class, and opinions about working alone or in small groups, understanding, achievement, and how interesting the class was. Student responses to the 14 questions were rated on a scale of one (least positive) to four (most positive).

An observation instrument was developed using the classroom seating chart and a time point observation procedure was used to identify whether each student was at task (attending to computer learning tasks) or off task (Acheson, 1980). Two observers were used on occasion to assure a reliable assessment. Over a period of 6 weeks, more than 60 ratings of at task behavior were possible for each class member.

A productivity instrument was devised to measure the amount of computer programming that each student group successfully completed. The instrument consisted of five progressively more difficult programs which students were to work through in five class sessions of 55 minutes each. The productivity score was determined by the number of programs each group was able to successfully complete.

RESULTS

A strong case can be made for students grouped as triads studying together at the computer. Not only did students studying in triads attain an equivalent (no statistically significant difference) achievement level, maintain equivalent levels of at-task behavior and display an equally positive attitude as pairs and individuals at the computer, but triads were superior to pairs in the productivity of computer programming (see Table 16). The concept that one student per computer is the ideal ratio was not the case in this evaluation. The use of trios at the computer was found to be equally as effective as having individuals at the computer.

The use of student grouping of trios offered a considerable cost reduction compared to individual use of the computer because it reduced the number of computers required. In addition, the use of traids provided the administrator with the flexibility to schedule full class units of 30 students, and potentially a whole student population to computer instruction if six week courses are instituted.

Table 16
Measurement of the Quality of Learning Within Three Grouping Arrangements

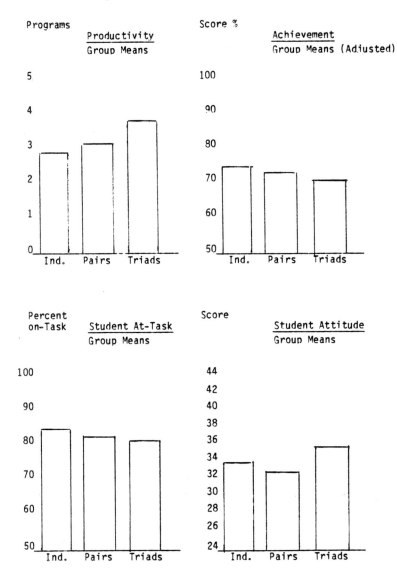

The conclusion of the evaluation was that students grouped at the computer in triads in computer programming classes achieved as well,

stayed at-task as well, and displayed as positive an attitude as groupings of pairs or individuals at the computer. Students grouped in triads, however, were superior (statistical significance) to pairs in the amount of computer programming that they completed. Groups of triads can provide an opportunity for computer instruction for more students at a lower cost, and without any sacrifice of student learning.

REFLECTIONS AND SECOND THOUGHTS

It was found that the evaluation of an on-going instructional program was rewarding because the results of the study had a direct application and meaning for the students, teachers, and administrators involved. These results, which were supportive of the instructional program, were an encouragement to those involved in the study. The pod concept now had some research support for its usage.

There were, of course, also times of discouragement associated with the evaluation. So much of the evaluation was dependent upon the cooperation of others and the controls exercised by the evaluator were only indirect. There were also those anxious moments arising from unexpected problems. One class in particular due to discipline problems would have been excluded from the study had not the problem been corrected. There was a constant worry about the number of students in each class. Could a workable balance of students in the control groups and experimental groups be maintained?

The use of the experimental design in the evaluation of an on-going instructional program is not as common as perhaps it should be. The area of curriculum evaluation certainly needs the kind of statistical evidence that the experimental design offers.

After the completion of this evaluation there was a definite feeling of accomplishment in finding that an evaluation of an experimental design could be successfully conducted in an existing instructional program without undue interruption to that program.

References

Acheson, K. A. and Gall, M. D. *Techniques in the Clinical Supervision of Teachers* New York: Longman Inc., 1980.

Hornsby, W. The pod concept in classroom networking. *TRS-80 Microcomputer News* Vol 5 (10), October, 1983, 14–15.

Life Skills: Introduction to Computers Teacher's Manual A517-SATC Society for Visual Education, Inc., SVE, Chicago: The Singer Company, 1981.

Spaulding, R. An Evaluation of Computer Programming Courses in a Junior High School Relating Student Grouping to the Quality of Learning *Dissertation Abstracts International,* 1985, Vol. 45 (07) P 1949-A.

APPENDIX A

AN ANNOTATED LIST OF INSTRUMENTS
FOR CURRICULUM EVALUATION

Learner

Scale Name: "Rating the Affective Domain"
Source: Hughes, Abby and Karen Frommer, A System for Monitoring Affective Objectives in *Educational Leadership* Alexandria Virginia: Association for Supervision and Curriculum Development, April, 1982, Vol. 39 No. 7 pp. 521–523.

Purpose: To profile individual students and entire classes on factor of personal and social behavior for pursuing objectives of a personal and social behavior.

Level: K–12

Method: Teacher observation checklist with 5 point likert scale items.

Time: no specified (brief)

Length: 70 Items

Scoring: Suitable for maintaining individual learner profile.

Scale Name: "Self-Responsibility Interview Schedule"

Source: Wang, Margaret C. and Billie Stiles, An Investigation of Children's Concept of Self-Responsibility for Their School Learning in *American Educational Research Journal* A.E.R.A. Summer 1976, Vol. 13, No. 3, pp. 159–179.

Purpose: Designed to obtain information about:
  a) student self-knowledge about learning;
  b) ability to self-evalute learning; and
  c) preference for self-managed or teacher managed learning.

Level: Primary students (adaptable for older students)

Method: Interview with young children, questionnaire with older learners.

Time: 10 minutes

Length: 18 Items

Scoring: Hand scoring

Scale Name: "Student Self-Report Checklist"
Source: Levin, Tamar with Ruth Long *Effective Instruction* Alexandria, Virginia: Association for Supervision and Curriculum Development, 1981. pp. 50.
Purpose: The checklist for describing activities and thoughts of students during class which relate to the research constructs of corrective feedback, instructional cues, and degree of involvement.
Level: Probably grades 7–12; perhaps intermediate levels of grades 4, 5, and 6 also.
Time: Suggested at the end of each lesson or two lessons.
Length: 25 Items; directions suggest shortening the items.
Scoring: Hand scoring.

Scale Name: "Junior Index of Motivation" (Jim Scale)
Source: Frymier, Jack R., *The Nature of Educational Method,* Columbus, Ohio: Charles E. Merrill, 1965 pp. 136–9.
Purpose: Measures high and low motivation to achieve in school.
Level: Grades 7–12
Method: Paper/pencil.
Time: 30 minutes
Length: 80 Items
Scoring: Hand scoring

Scale Name: "Time-on-Task Observation Form"

Source: Hosford, Philip L., The Art of Applying the Science of Education in *Using What We Know About Teaching* Alexandria, Virginia: Association for Supervision and Curriculum Development, pp. 150–152.

Purpose: To assess the percentage of on-task behavior of a class of students over a seven minute observation period.

Level: K–12

Method: Requires a visiting observer

Time: 7 minutes observation

Length: Seven total class observations (one per minute)

Scoring: Hand scoring (simple percentage)

Instruction

Scale Name: "A Questionnaire for Assessing the (Teacher) Expectancy Factor".

Source: Hosford, Philip L., "The Art of Applying the Science of Education", in *Using What We Know About Teaching*, Alexandria, Virginia: Association for Supervision and Curriculum Development, pp. 152–153.

Purpose: To assess the teacher's expectations as perceived by the students on assignment, enjoyment of learning, and cooperative learning.

Level: Grades 5–12

Method: Can be administered by teacher to students

Time: Not mentioned (brief)

Length: 3 Items

Scoring: Hand scoring

Scale Name: "Monitoring Index"

Source: Hosford, Philip L., The Art of Applying the Science of Education, in *Using What We Know About Teaching*, Alexandria, Virginia: Association for Supervision and Curriculum Development, pp. 153–156.

Purpose: Procedure may be used to assess the teacher's ability to predict student performance on tests, assignments, ability to do homework. Can identify problems of learners or readiness of class for assignment or tests.

Level: Used in grades 2–12.

Method: Prediction by teacher of each learner, actual results collected and compared.

Time: Brief

Length: Based on item length of assignment or test

Scoring: Hand scoring; percentage outcome

Scale Name: "Postclass Reactions"

Source: Fox, Robert, et al., *Diagnosing Classroom Learning Environments* Chicago: Science Research Associates, 1966, pp. 17–19.

Purpose: To diagnose pupils' reactions to specific learning experiences.

Level: K–12 (variation shown for primary level)

Method: Can be read to younger learners, show of hands, or individual reaction sheets.

Time: A few minutes at the end of a class session or lesson

Length: 7 Items (each may be followed by open-ended responses)

Scoring: Hand scored by teacher or pupils

Scale Name: "Teacher Self Evaluation Checklist"

Source: Levin, Tamar with Ruth Long, *Effective Instruction,* Alexandria Virginia: Association for Supervision and Curriculum Development—1981, pp. 47–50.

Purpose: The checklist can be used by teachers to evaluate their instructional and management effectiveness on research validated constructs of corrective feedback, instructional cues, and student involvement.

Level: Teacher self-administered, K–12

Method:

Time: Not indicated (a few minutes perhaps) suggested for use at the end of a lesson or a school day.

Length: 45 items

Scoring: Hand scoring

Scale Name: "Signs of Creative Teaching and Assessment Procedures"

Source: Leeper, Robert R., ed., *Humanistic Education: Objectives and Assessment,* Washington, D.C.: Association Supervision and Curriculum Development 1978, pp. 32–37.

Purpose: To assess the 14 signs of creative teaching and learning for humanistic education.

Level: All levels

Method: Observation

Time: Varied

Length: Not specific

Score: Hand scored; ratio statistic

Scale Name: "Transaction Ability Inventory"

Source: Gregorc, Anthony F., Learning/Teaching Styles: Their Nature and Effects, in *Student Learning Styles: Diagnosing and Prescribing Programs*, Ed., James W. Keeke, Reston, Va: National Association of Secondary School Principals 1979 pp. 19–26.

Purpose: Matching learning style with instructional materials and methods.

Level: Junior High/adult

Method: Paper/pencil, observation and interview may be used

Time: 5 minutes

Length: 10 sets of 4 items

Scoring: Hand scoring

Scale Name: "Classroom Observation Schedule"

Source: Fox, Robert, et al., *Diagnosing Classroom Learning Environments*, Chicago: Science Research Associates, 1966, pp. 55–57.

Purpose: A system for recording instances of work and social and control behavior by both teacher and learners during a single class period.

Level: K–12 (however actual examples are from high school level)

Method: Requires an independent observer. Needs a recording sheet prepared before the observation.

Time: As little as 5 minutes to an entire class period

Length: Recording of three different symbols within 13 categories

Scoring: Interpreting directly from the recording sheet

Staff Development

Scale Name: "Staff Development Programming Principal's Checklist"
Source: Rogers, Joseph F., Building an Effective Staff Development Program: A Principal's Checklist, in *NASSP BULLETIN* Reston, Va: National Association of Secondary School Principals, Vol. 67, No. 461, March 1983, pp. 9–11.
Purpose: For review of a staff development program to identify needs for planning and improvement.
Level: K–12
Method: Self-scored checklist
Time: brief
Length: 30 Items
Scoring: Interpretations may be drawn directly from checklist items and catagories of items.

Scale Name: "Perspective of Man Combined with Categories of Ex-
.pectations"

Source: Longstreet, Wilma S., *Beyond Jenks: The Myth of Equal Schooling* Washington, D.C.: Association for Supervision and Curriculum Development, 1973, pp. 21.

Purpose: Can be used to analyze school philosophy statements and
written description of specific curricular designs. Reveals
the philosophical bias and the educational priorities of a
curriculum design.

Level: Curriculum design at any level

Method: Best done by group interaction of professional educators,
Matrix and curriculum must be reviewed thoroughly.

Time: 30 to 45 minutes

Length: Matrix of 5 × 6 categories

Scoring: Interpretations can be drawn directly from the matrix

Scale Name: "Looking at Ourselves and Our Schools"
Source: Beane, James A., and R. P. Lipka, *Self Concept, Self Esteem, and the Curriculum,* Boston: Allyn and Bacon, 1984, pp. 201–205.
Purpose: To assess ideas, beliefs, programs, practices about enhancing learner self-concept in the school.
Level: School level by faculty, administration, counselor
Method: Survey (also described in an interview process with learners), pp. 209–215
Time: Not indicated
Length: 3 checklists; 86 items in all
Scoring: Hand scoring

Scale Name: "Questionnaire for Assessing School and Classroom Effectiveness"

Source: Squires, David A., et al., *Effective Schools and Classrooms: A Research Based Perspective*, Washington, D.C., Association for Supervision and Curriculum Development 1983, pp. 91–103.

Purpose: For faculty of a school to summarize their perceptions of the accomplishments and needs for an effective school.

Level: Can be used at: school level by faculty; district level by administrators; and board level

Method: Survey opinionare

Time: 30–40 minutes

Length: 60 Items

Score: Hand scoring

Curricular Materials

Scale Name: "Questionnaire for Analyzing Instructional and Learning Materials"

Source: Levin, Tamar with Ruth Long, *Effective Instruction,* Alexandria, Virginia: Association for Supervision and Curriculum Development, 1981, pp. 52–53.

Purpose: To analyze instructional materials on the research concepts of feedback, cues, and degree of involvement. Enables assignment of some students to independent work; reveals a need for additional materials preparation.

Level: K–12 and adult

Time: Brief; suggested use during lesson planning

Length: 28 Items

Scoring: Hand scoring

APPENDIX B

TABLE OF RANDOM NUMBERS

1353	6755	3353	4316	0723	0491	1434	7403	5530	1551	4536	8258
1030	6490	4665	4583	0508	6797	1213	0234	0977	8753	8719	8540
9842	8159	5377	3826	9564	7949	6622	5306	0176	8301	3225	9637
2141	5135	6538	8013	4236	8294	6641	3650	1536	1367	9376	8948
9639	5989	4178	6167	4400	5896	0774	6705	7810	1517	3809	4200
0771	3838	1086	6971	7046	4537	8806	8648	4341	3220	5247	7500
6526	7588	1788	7434	3514	9175	8424	9881	3276	5728	9880	2728
5515	8382	5654	3487	5032	3807	2554	1321	7674	9155	0865	7791
0035	1550	3987	4971	8936	3879	7850	6866	2668	9217	6284	9752
6216	8297	8836	3343	5537	8135	3977	9014	3565	5266	4510	4663
3445	7720	0308	7371	6448	7354	1084	3440	3330	4014	9114	3553
3967	6863	0473	6070	7156	3304	0420	0320	7796	8897	8214	4211
3790	7190	4031	4477	5582	8191	3909	9136	3855	5901	5713	6163
1113	1114	1662	4949	9732	8843	0476	5083	9898	8640	7757	3779
1849	2305	2188	7385	9617	6235	5855	7235	4087	4410	4675	3362
1247	1829	4746	7012	4358	8035	3989	4397	3152	4341	2671	1960
2154	6658	5560	8438	5587	2580	0203	4766	5120	2820	5845	4683
9214	3541	3318	3040	3379	7911	2053	0605	4590	7092	6238	8599
2986	5093	8677	1228	4271	9570	3985	2513	9297	8165	0315	3406
1106	4529	2222	7564	0388	9251	7012	7302	4993	9238	5489	4788
6378	3704	9822	0600	0201	0798	7982	5439	0342	8098	0506	5151
4268	6827	7551	8865	0229	6588	2458	3499	6006	9542	8196	8299
8109	9834	1026	2649	1658	1108	6724	4089	6605	7822	2491	9544
7293	6214	6650	8975	8997	8201	3237	4976	3874	3460	0889	9190
7711	2078	8070	4717	0674	6594	8494	7446	4488	4910	4065	5205
0024	2222	8113	3675	4033	6124	5442	2605	2700	7750	7195	8421
8465	0278	0484	5398	3030	4600	5323	6604	7274	9204	4761	0730
3557	8133	1782	2496	3933	6136	6416	3418	3577	5692	6958	5523
7166	2632	6295	9080	2825	3718	2991	3906	1993	1799	7860	5962
3332	6209	2261	2681	0740	7769	4753	8196	8848	4317	1272	3777
9620	8430	9002	3140	2818	3794	1031	2947	9427	5039	0391	1994
6182	7569	4778	5545	5269	4305	0298	1470	2107	4407	2480	0215
7913	4248	9268	2375	5838	5920	2723	8569	4107	2517	3138	1172
1394	3519	3564	4717	1223	2774	4143	1521	8198	0494	4177	5618
1578	8679	2874	4131	3917	2441	5098	6868	4315	9077	0630	7087
8814	3589	7214	5980	5947	3958	8633	0381	3215	0857	1206	4517
3895	1567	9351	7000	2835	6951	8939	5186	2081	0813	1150	4585
9534	1062	5571	8863	8035	2388	7361	3831	4502	7530	9661	5193
1895	4006	1980	0825	2125	4292	8775	2117	3187	5068	6729	9758
5898	2969	9729	6649	7329	6346	5171	1402	0652	6292	6885	9678
6360	8340	7794	6702	5066	0559	2889	7505	7164	0437	3147	9951
1501	0091	2031	6368	4924	7862	8157	6375	1509	6675	1472	3753
1822	8162	7571	6973	8692	3096	3311	2444	7293	6763	9937	3757
1186	6959	6072	8802	3164	2718	3662	5782	8167	1961	3267	6949
6561	8315	5845	5232	3782	0495	5823	9277	0606	5139	0379	1020
1047	1853	6694	8482	5642	0445	0281	0403	2969	9180	3362	2547
2608	4895	0896	6323	4869	2602	9957	1599	7884	7910	1504	2834

Reproduced by permission of the publisher, F. E. Peacock Publishers, Inc., Itasca, IL. From John Mordechai Gottman and Robert Earl Clasen, *Evaluation in Education: A Practitioner's Guide*, 1972, p. 356.

APPENDIX C

Synopsis of standards For Evaluations of Educational Programs,
Projects, and Materials by The Joint Committee on
Standards for Education Evaluation, 1981.

A. Utility Standards

The Utility Standards are intended to ensure that an evaluation will
serve the practical information needs of given audiences. These standards are:

A1 Audience Identification

Audiences involved in or affected by the evaluation should be
identified, so that their needs can be addressed.

A2 Evaluator Credibility

The persons conducting the evaluation should be both trustworthy
and competent to perform the evaluation, so that their findings
achieve maximum credibility and acceptance.

A3 Information Scope and Selection

Information collected should be of such scope and selected in such
ways as to address pertinent questions about the object of the
evaluation and be responsive to the needs and interests of specific
audiences.

A4 Valuational Interpretation

The perspectives, procedures, and rationale used to interpret the
findings should be carefully described, so that the bases for value
judgments are clear.

A5 Report Clarity

The evaluation report should describe the object being evaluated and its context, and the purposes, procedures, and findings
of the evaluation, so that the audiences will readily understand
what was done, why it was done, what information was obtained,
what conclusions were drawn, and what recommendations were
made.

A6   **Report Dissemination**
Evaluation findings should be disseminated to clients and other
right-to-know audiences, so that they can assess and use the findings.

A7   **Report Timeliness**
Release of reports should be timely, so that audiences can best use
the reported information.

A8   **Evaluation Impact**
Evaluations should be planned and conducted in ways that encourage follow-through by members of the audiences.

B.   Feasibility Standards

The Feasibility Standards are intended to ensure that an evaluation
will be realistic, prudent, diplomatic, and frugal; they are:

B1   **Practical Procedures**
The evaluation procedures should be practical, so that disruption
is kept to a minimum, and that needed information can be obtained.

B2   **Political Viability**
The evaluation should be planned and conducted with anticipation of the different positions of various interest groups, so that
their cooperation may be obtained, and so that possible attempts by
any of these groups to curtail evaluation operations or to bias or
misapply the results can be averted or counteracted.

B3   **Cost Effectiveness**
The evaluation should produce information of sufficient value to
justify the resources expended.

C.   Propriety Standards

The Propriety Standards are intended to ensure that an evaluation
will be conducted legally, ethically, and with due regard for the welfare
of those involved in the evaluation, as well as those affected by its results.
These standards are:

C1   **Formal Obligation**
Obligations of the formal parties to an evaluation (what is to be
done, how, by whom, when) should be agreed to in writing, so that
these parties are obligated to adhere to all conditions of the agreement or formally to renegotiate it.

C2   **Conflict of Interest**
Conflict of interest, frequently unavoidable, should be dealt with
openly and honestly, so that it does not compromise the evaluation
processes and results.

C3 **Full and Frank Disclosure**
Oral and written evaluation reports should be open, direct, and honest in their disclosure of pertinent findings, including the limitations of the evaluation.

C4 **Public's Right to Know**
The formal parties to an evaluation should respect and assure the public's right to know, within the limits of other related principles and statutes, such as those dealing with public safety and the right to privacy.

C5 **Rights of Human Subjects**
Evaluations should be designed and conducted, so that the rights and welfare of the human subjects are respected and protected.

C6 **Human Interactions**
Evaluators should respect human dignity and worth in their interactions with other persons associated with an evaluation.

C7 **Balanced Reporting**
The evaluation should be complete and fair in its presentation of strengths and weaknesses of the object under investigation, so that strengths can be built upon and problem areas addressed.

C8 **Fiscal Responsibility**
The evaluator's allocation and expenditure of resources should reflect sound accountability procedures and otherwise be prudent and ethically responsible.

D. Accuracy Standards
The Accuracy Standards are intended to ensure that an evaluation will reveal and convey technically adequate information about the features of the object being studied that determine its worth or merit. These standards are:

D1 **Object Identification**
The object of the evaluation (program, project, material) should be sufficiently examined, so that the form(s) of the object being considered in the evaluation can be clearly identified.

D2 **Context Analysis**
The context in which the program, project, or material exists should be examined in enough detail, so that its likely influences on the object can be identified.

D3 **Described Purposes and Procedures**
The purposes and procedures of the evaluation should be monitored

and described in enough detail, so that they can be identified and assessed.

D4   *Defensible Information Sources*
The sources of information should be described in enough detail, so that the adequacy of the information can be assessed.

D5   *Valid Measurement*
The information-gathering instruments and procedures should be chosen or developed and then implemented in ways that will assure that the interpretation arrived at is valid for the given use.

D6   *Reliable Measurement*
The information-gathering instruments and procedures should be chosen or developed and then implemented in ways that will assure that the information obtained is sufficiently reliable for the intended use.

D7   *Systematic Data Control*
The data collected, processed, and reported in an evaluation should be reviewed and corrected, so that the results of the evaluation will not be flawed.

D8   *Analysis of Quantitative Information*
Quantitative information in an evaluation should be appropriately and systematically analyzed to ensure supportable interpretations.

D9   *Analysis of Quanlitative Information*
Qualitative information in an evaluation should be appropriately and systematically analyzed to ensure supportable interpretations.

D10 *Justified Conclusions*
The conclusions reached in an evaluation should be explicitly justified, so that the audiences can assess them.

D11 *Objective Reporting*
The evaluation procedures should provide safeguards to protect the evaluation findings and reports against distortion by the personal feelings and biases of any party to the evaluation.

INDEX